haXe 2
Beginner's Guide

Develop exciting applications with this multi-platform
programming language

Benjamin Dasnois

BIRMINGHAM - MUMBAI

haxe 2
Beginner's Guide

First published: July 2011

Production Reference: 1180711

Published by Packt Publishing Ltd.
32 Lincoln Road
Olton
Birmingham, B27 6PA, UK.

ISBN 978-1-849512-56-5

www.packtpub.com

Cover Image by Asher Wishkerman (a.wishkerman@mpic.de)

Credits

Author
Benjamin Dasnois

Reviewers
Marcus Bergström
Andy Li
Franco Ponticelli

Acquisition Editor
Dilip Venkatesh

Development Editor
Maitreya Bhakal

Technical Editors
Kavita Iyer
Azharuddin Sheikh

Copy Editor
Neha Shetty

Project Coordinator
Shubhanjan Chatterjee

Proofreader
Lisa Brady

Indexer
Tejal Daruwale

Production Coordinator
ArvindKumar Gupta

Cover Work
ArvindKumar Gupta

Foreword

Remember the olden days?

I vaguely remember this odd box called a computer gradually conquering corners of my living room and bedroom. Can you recall those times? We would "use a computer" for some specific tasks, such as writing a letter.

The term computer was quite popular back then. Now, the word is no longer part of our active vocabulary, let alone "use a computer", who says that anymore? Nobody does. That is because computers are no longer odd boxes in corners. They are the notebooks and mobile phones that we use every day. They are also the hybrids between the two, such as tablets and netbooks. They are the servers that run websites we constantly use as well. Even today's TVs are full-blown computers.

I find this change fascinating. I think we live in a very exciting time to be participating in the business. All these new devices bring us opportunities enabling us to express our creativity, while their differences challenge us and keep us inventive.

Unlike PHP or ActionScript, haXe is not designed for one specific purpose. It is just a programming language. That is why it is so versatile. Whether it is the hip new phone in the hands of a Japanese ad girl or a big bulky machine in a server room; whether it has a mouse, a multi-touch screen, a bendable/deformable interface; or even a mind reading sensor, haXe can be remixed and used for the device.

This means that you can use the same language and even the same codebase across the browser and the server part of your project, for example. To me, that is why haXe is so relevant.

Benjamin Dasnois is one of the people that has been around since haXe-day one. He remixes haXe to make it fit new needs. Benjamin is best known within the community for working on the Java target. (I would also say, that he is second to none for his funny French accent.)

In this book, Benjamin will introduce you to the world of haXe. Once you get to the last page, you will have the skill set to start developing for a browser and a big bulky server using the same language.

However, remember: a programming language is never your goal; it is a tool that assists you in achieving your goal, be it creating awesome software that enriches all of our lives or helping us achieve world domination.

Pimm Hogeling
haXe Developer and Interface Designer

About the Author

Benjamin Dasnois has always been fascinated by open source software and as such, has been giving courses about Linux in an IT school in France. In the meantime, Benjamin has been following and working with haXe since its beginning and uses it in his professional life. He now works on an open source project, started the integration of haXe into it, and made it work with the technologies that were already in use.

I would like to thank the entire haXe community, my schoolmates, and former students who really made me discover the contribution I could make by imparting my knowledge or communicating my skills.

About the Reviewers

Marcus Bergström is the Technical Director and a co-owner of the digital creative studio Quickform. Working on a day-to-day basis with projects, spanning everything from websites to business applications, he knows the importance of choosing the right tool for the job. With a portfolio packed with world known brands, quality assurance is paramount, as well as production speed.

As one of the early adopters of the language, Marcus has been using haXe as his secret weapon while spearheading all the developments of haXe within the company for years. His favorite features include the strict typing and the ability to write both client and server-side applications in one language.

His business is located in the sunny south of Spain where he lives with his wife and two children. He believes that Sundays are best enjoyed with a cold beer after a good round of golf with friends.

Andy Li is a haXe developer in Hong Kong, with a Bachelor's Degree (first class honors) in Creative Media from City University of Hong Kong. He is now a PhD student in the School of Creative Media, City University of Hong Kong, researching in the fields of computer vision, computer graphics, and installation art.

He has been actively involved in the haXe community, producing several open source haXe libraries, including CasaHx (haXe port of CasaLib for AS3), hxColorToolkit (toolkit for managing colors), hxOpenFrameworks (haXe binding to openFrameworks), and jQueryExtern (haXe extern file for jQuery).

His personal blog, `http://blog.onthewings.net/`, contains many open source experiments and programming tips.

Franco Ponticelli is an experienced software developer and a problem solver. An Architecture graduate with specialization in Industrial Design, he performs many different activities in the Information Technology area from 3D computer graphics to hard-core software development. In his constant research for the perfect development environment, he found haXe and fell in love with it.

He is the author of the book *Professional haXe and Neko* published by Wrox.

I would like to thank my wife and kids for their support.

www.PacktPub.com

Support files, eBooks, discount offers and more

You might want to visit www.PacktPub.com for support files and downloads related to your book.

Did you know that Packt offers eBook versions of every book published, with PDF and ePub files available? You can upgrade to the eBook version at www.PacktPub.com and as a print book customer, you are entitled to a discount on the eBook copy. Get in touch with us at service@packtpub.com for more details.

At www.PacktPub.com, you can also read a collection of free technical articles, sign up for a range of free newsletters and receive exclusive discounts and offers on Packt books and eBooks.

http://PacktLib.PacktPub.com

Do you need instant solutions to your IT questions? PacktLib is Packt's online digital book library. Here, you can access, read and search across Packt's entire library of books.

Why subscribe?

- ◆ Fully searchable across every book published by Packt
- ◆ Copy and paste, print and bookmark content
- ◆ On demand and accessible via web browser

Free access for Packt account holders

If you have an account with Packt at www.PacktPub.com, you can use this to access PacktLib today and view nine entirely free books. Simply use your login credentials for immediate access.

Table of Contents

Preface

haXe is the universal programming language which is completely cross-platform and provides a standard library that remains the same—regardless of platform.

haXe 2 Beginner's Guide will get you up and running with this exciting language and will guide you through its features in the easiest way possible.

haXe has filled the gap in creating multi-platform applications, and this book will fill the gap in learning all you need to know about haXe—even if it is the first time you have heard of it.

This book will enable you to fully realize haXe's potential for translating code from a haXe program into different languages.

Start with learning how to install haXe, work your way up to templating, and finally learn how to make the same code work for multiple platforms. In between, find heaps of tricks and techniques and work with haXe's typing system. Learn about inheritance, go from learning what a parameter is to creating your own parameterized classes, and find out what the fuss is all about regarding the dynamic type.

By the time you are done with this book, you will find yourself writing efficient haXe code for multiple platforms in less time than you can say "compatible".

Here is haXe

haXe started as a web-oriented programming language and has gone a long way since its debut in late 2005. Its main goal was to correct several big issues within web development, but now people and companies are using it to be able to cover several platforms and devices.

Where and for what is haXe used?

Well, it seems like you are interested in haXe, and we will soon write our first haXe program together. However, before doing that, you may be wondering who uses haXe, and for what kind of tasks or applications it is used.

Where is haXe used?

haXe is actually used in several places. There are some companies that are using it for their professional work. That does not necessarily mean that they use haXe for their whole work; many companies that uses haXe are indeed going through a move towards haXe, or are simply using haXe for some parts of their work and do not necessarily plan to use it more. Even though haXe is not difficult to learn, it is really difficult to change the technologies a company is using.

There are also several open source projects that use haXe. For example, haXe libraries are written in haXe, and many of these are open source.

There are also hobbyists, or students, who are learning and using haXe. Learning haXe and participating in the community helps in learning many programming concepts (the community sometime talks about some people that are not in haXe at the moment but may be added later, for example.) It is also advantageous to learn something other than what is usually taught in schools.

What is haXe used for?

haXe is used for a lot of different things. At first, it is mainly used for making website-related things. This can be web-based tools (such as a mind-mapping program), or games in Flash or JavaScript.

It can also be used for writing desktop applications. Some people have been using a great combination of Flash and Neko to achieve this. However, this is not the only way to do things! You can write command-line applications that will not need Flash, or you can use or write another graphic library.

One can write servers with haXe too. The framework provides some helpers to do that. One impressive example of a server written in haXe is haXeVideo available at `http://code.google.com/p/haxevideo/`. This is a video server that allows live streaming of videos to Flash clients. Although it is not ready for production at the moment, it is a great start and can put you on the right track.

haXe can be used to directly target mobile devices such as iOS and Android, but it's also possible to use it to write web-based applications targeting mobile devices. Nowadays, many phones have a browser that is able to run JavaScript code. There are also some runtimes that allow one to create applications based on web technologies running on mobile devices.

One language to rule them all

If you have already been developing web applications, then you certainly know how painful it is to switch from, say, PHP, to JavaScript and Flash. In fact, even the most basic things can become painful in such a scheme. For example, switching from one language to another can make adding objects to an array or a list difficult and error-prone while developing web applications.

haXe is there to unify the development of the three main parts of web applications; with it, you will be able to write your server-code, your client-code, and your rich-client code with only one language: haXe. However, it is also possible to use it with other languages.

Object-oriented programming

haXe also brings the oriented-object programming concept with the well-known principle of classes to platforms that do not natively support it. This way, you will be able to create a program using the well-known concepts of classes, types (also with generics), enums, and others even if this program runs in the browser.

haXe versions

haXe's version 1 was made available in 2006, but since 2008, we have been using haXe 2. haXe 2 brought several changes both to the language and to the library. Therefore, this is the version we're going to learn together. When you get familiar with haXe, you will understand that haXe is a very fast evolving language and sometimes, even minor versions may bring some important new features. This allows haXe to bring you more and more power as time goes by, but keep in mind that it may sometime (although this is very rare) break your code.

Note that in this book, we are using haXe Version **2.0.6**.

At the beginning of haXe, only the Flash and Neko targets were available. This means that haXe code could only be compiled to be run on Flash (AVM indeed, as that is the name of the virtual machine) or on the Neko virtual machine. Some weeks after, the already-announced Javascript target made its appearance, but with limited support (particularly in regards to closures). Nowadays, the Javascript target is really mature and can be used without any major problems. Later on, new versions of Flash were supported. All of these targets and the base of the compiler were due to Nicolas Cannasse from Motion-Twin. He is the genius mind behind haXe.

The first target that had been created by someone else was the PHP target. Franco Ponticelli released it hoping that people would experience with it, as it is much easier to get a PHP host than a Neko host. Since then, the PHP target has evolved and has become very mature and may be used in a production environment.

In 2009, the C++ generator was developed by Hugh Sanderson. This target creates C++ code from your haXe code. You can then compile it with a C++ compiler, such as GCC. Beware that it is still under heavy work. Hugh Sanderson is famous in the haXe community for making possible the development of games for iPhone and Android with haXe.

Some people are working on implementing other targets. At the time of writing this book, we know about a Java target in development by yours truly.

Also, note that even though it is not really a target on its own, it is now possible to use the Javascript target to write applications that are to be run on NodeJS.

haXe and the new models of web applications

Nowadays, we see many new and exciting web applications that are using a model that is quite new where the following three parts are communicating together:

1. The server.
2. The client-side with Flash.
3. The client-side with Javascript.

It is usually quite difficult to make those three parts communicate because each language has its own structure. With haXe, as you are using the same language everywhere, you do not have to switch between structures.

In addition, haXe has support for its own remoting; this is a way to allow you to communicate between several haXe applications as seamlessly as possible through the network or between a JavaScript and a Flash application running in the same page.

Some people have also implemented haXeRemoting in other languages making it possible to communicate with applications written in those languages.

haXe as an universal language

Nowadays, haXe can be used in order to do much more than just assisting with web applications. It can now be used in order to create, for example, applications for the iPhone or Android devices or for desktops.

In order to do so, a part of the Flash API has been implemented and made available when targeting C++. This way, it is possible to use this well-known API to create games on Windows, Linux, MacOSX, iPhone, and Android.

Getting help

As you will gain experience with haXe, you will surely encounter new problems to solve. This is an interesting part of programming, but if you find yourself really blocked, then there are several ways to get help.

Reading some documentation

There is some documentation available on the haXe website (`http://www.haxe.org/doc`) and you can also find the up-to-date API documentation at `http://www.haxe.org/api`. By the way, the haXe website is a wiki, which means that once you have registered, and when you have enough experience with haXe, you will be able to contribute to the documentation by modifying it or adding some new pages to it. You can also contribute by translating pages into your own language.

Asking questions

At some point, you will certainly want to talk with people about your problems and queries, or maybe share your thoughts about haXe. There are two main places to do that—the haXe forum and the haXe mailing list.

The haXe forum

Once you have registered an account on the haXe wiki, you can use it to post your questions on the haXe forum accessible at `http://www.haxe.org/forum`. This forum has been created primarily for newcomers who are generally more comfortable with such tools. There, you have great chances of finding other newcomers and also some haXe experts to help you.

The haXe mailing list

The mailing list was the first place where the community grew. Nowadays, it is where most haXe experts are, but they are also pleased to help newcomers there. On the mailing list, people ask questions to solve their problems, but it is also a place to discuss the language and tools evolution. The mailing list can be joined by going to `http://lists.motion-twin.com/mailman/listinfo/haxe`. If you want to know what is going to happen in the next versions of haXe, this is the place to be.

Some advice

Before you ask a question on the mailing list or on the forum, here is some advice.

- First of all, always be polite and humble, particularly since you are a new comer.
- Do not hesitate to introduce yourself in your first message (telling people who you are will help them to identify you, making you part of the community)

- Always explain what you are trying to achieve. This point is to help people help you. If they know what you are trying to achieve, they will know better how to assist you.

- Keep in mind that not all participants are native English speakers. Indeed, there are chances that most of them are not. Try to express yourself in an easy-to-understand way.

- Stay focused on one problem (or one group of linked problems) per thread. If you have several very different problems, create several threads.

- Always say what platform you are targeting (PHP, Flash, Neko, Javascript, and so on). Some problems may be platform specific.

- If you have a problem with some code, always try to reduce it to the smallest possible snippet that still reproduces the problem.

- If you send some code, always try to make it easily understandable. People who are trying to help are generally happy to do so, but if they have to guess what the variable is because you named it "avhgk" instead of "userName", they will sense that you are not even trying to help them help you.

Reading some blogs

There are many people who write about haXe on their own blog.

Nicolas Cannasse

Nicolas Cannasse, haXe's creator, maintains his own blog at `http://www.ncannasse.fr` where he discusses new and future things in haXe and its ecosystem, Flash, but also about the IT world.

Weblob

`http://www.weblob.net` is Franco Ponticelli's blog. Should I remind you that Franco Ponticelli is the PHP target creator? Although this is a low-traffic blog, you will find many interesting articles about haXe on it.

GameHaXe

Hugh Sanderson, the creator of the C++ target, maintains his blog located at `http://www.gamehaxe.com`. You will find some of his thoughts about haXe, the IT world, and experiments about game development in haXe.

He also explains how one can use haXe to target iOS and Android.

A Bug's Life

The author's blog, located at `http://www.benjamindasnois.com`, is where he talks about haXe. As he is also developing a Java target for haXe, he also writes a lot about it.

Blog.haxe.org

On `http://blog.haxe.org`, you can find an aggregate of several blogs about haXe. Some of them we have already discussed.

Helping the community

When you have some experience with haXe, you will certainly feel the need to participate in the community and help, as you have been helped. There are several ways to do this.

The mailing list and the forum

At first, and that is certainly the most obvious part, you can answer people's questions on the mailing list and on the forum.

If you do so, do not hesitate to give some advice. Share you experience—people who are migrating from the same language as you (if you are migrating) may want to hear about your experience.

Another way of participating on the mailing list is by making some proposals. If you think that you have a great idea that can make haXe even better, or can help newcomers, or everyday development with haXe, then you should propose it. People will tell you what they think about your idea and will eventually help you to make them come true.

The wiki

You can register on the wiki and write on it. There are several things that are needed on the wiki:

◆ Tutorials

◆ Updating the documentation according to changes

◆ Updating the documentation to reflect important things said on the mailing list

◆ Translating into your own language

Write on your blog or website

If you have a blog or a website, then you can write about haXe and your haXe experience on it. People always want to know how others have made the switch and how well it went. Having several sites talking about haXe helps spread the word too. Moreover, you can explain how you achieved a task and write a tutorial.

Writing libraries or tools

You can also write some libraries or tools and share them. As a developer, you will certainly use someone else's library at some point just because it is useless to rewrite things if they are already written well. So, think that someone else may also be interested in your work and distributing your libraries or tools is a great way to give back to the community.

You can also correct bugs in the haXe library and help maintaining libraries, so that they stay compatible with new versions of haXe.

You can find some libraries on `http://lib.haxe.org`.

Talking about haXe

Maybe, you are part of an association of programmers, or you are a student in an IT oriented school, or even a teacher. If this is the case, then maybe you can organize some conferences to talk about haXe. It is difficult to get people to know about a new and young language, such as haXe, because schools do not teach it and not many sites are talking about those languages.

Some people are already organizing such events (sometimes, even with workshops) and the more there are, the better it will be, because people will at least know about haXe and they can then decide if they want to use it or not (I do believe they will want to use it!).

If haXe is well-known, then you will certainly have more opportunities to use it.

What this book covers

Chapter 1, Getting to know haXe. In this chapter, you will be learning about haXe's history along with how to install it. You will also get some important information about how you can interact with the haXe community.

Chapter 2, Basic Syntax and *Branching*. In this chapter, you will learn about the basics of the haXe syntax. You will also learn how to make your programs behave differently depending on the situation.

Chapter 3, Being Cross-platform with haXe. In this chapter, you will learn how your code can be used to create programs that are going to run on several platforms.

Chapter 4, Understanding Types. In this chapter, you will learn about haXe's typing system.

Chapter 5, The Dynamic Type and Properties. In this chapter, you will learn about the Dynamic type. You will also learn how you can give your objects some properties.

Chapter 6, Using and Writing Interfaces, Typedefs, and Enums. In this chapter, you will learn what interfaces, typedefs, and enums are and how you can use them to improve your code.

Chapter 7, Communication Between haXe Programs. In this chapter, you will learn how to get your different haXe programs to communicate together by using haXeRemoting.

Chapter 8, Accessing Databases. In this chapter, you will learn how to access, read, and write to and from databases.

Chapter 9, Templating. In this chapter, you will learn how one can use templating in haXe to create, for example, views.

Chapter 10, Interfacing with the Target Platform. In this chapter, you will learn how you can access native functions and features from the platform you are targeting.

Chapter 11, A Dynamic Website Using Javascript. In this chapter, you will learn how you can use Javascript to create a website.

Chapter 12, Creating a Game with haXe and Flash. In this chapter, you will be guided through the creation of a game.

Appendix. In this section, we provide answers to the pop quiz.

What you need for this book

In order to run the code from this book, you will need the following:

- The haXe compiler
- The Neko runtime (it is installed with haXe if you use the haXe installer)
- A PHP capable web server (you can use solutions such as WAMP/XAMP on Windows or MAMP on MacOSX)
- A MySQL server (included in solutions named before)
- SWFMill (http://swfmill.org/):

Who this book is for

This book is written for both beginners and developers who want to learn this multi-platform programming language to build web applications from scratch.

Conventions

In this book, you will find several headings appearing frequently.

To give clear instructions of how to complete a procedure or task, we use:

Time for action – heading

1.   Action 1

2.   Action 2

3.   Action 3

Instructions often need some extra explanation so that they make sense, so they are followed with:

What just happened?

This heading explains the working of tasks or instructions that you have just completed.

You will also find some other learning aids in the book, including:

Pop quiz – heading

These are short multiple choice questions intended to help you test your own understanding.

Have a go hero – heading

These set practical challenges and give you ideas for experimenting with what you have learned.

You will also find a number of styles of text that distinguish between different kinds of information. Here are some examples of these styles, and an explanation of their meaning.

Code words in text are shown as follows: "You can verify that haXe is correctly installed by opening a terminal and running the `haxe` command; if haXe is correctly installed, then you should get the help message."

A block of code is set as follows:

```
class Main
{
    public static function main()
    {
        trace("Hello World");
    }
}
```

When we wish to draw your attention to a particular part of a code block, the relevant lines or items are set in bold:

```
class TesthaXe
{
    public static function main(): Void
    {
        var e = new EReg("^Hello.*",""); //Creates an EReg matching any
            string beginning with Hello
        if(e.match("Hello Benjamin"))
        {
            neko.Lib.println("Matches");
        } else
        {
            neko.Lib.println("Does not match");
        }
    }
}
```

Any command-line input or output is written as follows:

```
X-Cache : MISS from rack1.tumblr.com

X-Cache-Lookup : MISS from rack1.tumblr.com:80

Via : 1.0 rack1.tumblr.com:80 (squid/2.6.STABLE6)

P3P : CP="ALL ADM DEV PSAi COM OUR OTRo STP IND ONL"

Set-Cookie : tmgioct=h6NSbuBBgVV2IH3qzPEPPQLg; expires=Thu, 02-Jul-
    2020 23:30:11
```

New terms and **important words** are shown in bold. Words that you see on the screen, in menus, or dialog boxes for example, appear in the text like this: "Go to http://www.haxe.org and click on the **Download** link".

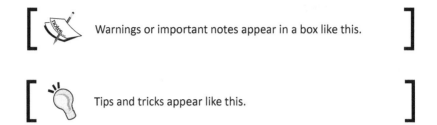

Warnings or important notes appear in a box like this.

Tips and tricks appear like this.

Reader feedback

Feedback from our readers is always welcome. Let us know what you think about this book—what you liked or may have disliked. Reader feedback is important for us to develop titles that you really get the most out of.

To send us general feedback, simply send an e-mail to feedback@packtpub.com, and mention the book title via the subject of your message.

If there is a book that you need and would like to see us publish, please send us a note in the **SUGGEST A TITLE** form on www.packtpub.com or e-mail suggest@packtpub.com.

If there is a topic that you have expertise in and you are interested in either writing or contributing to a book, see our author guide on www.packtpub.com/authors.

Customer support

Now that you are the proud owner of a Packt book, we have a number of things to help you to get the most from your purchase.

Downloading the example code for this book

You can download the example code files for all Packt books you have purchased from your account at http://www.PacktPub.com. If you purchased this book elsewhere, you can visit http://www.PacktPub.com/support and register to have the files e-mailed directly to you.

Errata

Although we have taken every care to ensure the accuracy of our content, mistakes do happen. If you find a mistake in one of our books—maybe a mistake in the text or the code—we would be grateful if you would report this to us. By doing so, you can save other readers from frustration and help us improve subsequent versions of this book. If you find any errata, please report them by visiting `http://www.packtpub.com/support`, selecting your book, clicking on the **errata submission form** link, and entering the details of your errata. Once your errata are verified, your submission will be accepted and the errata will be uploaded on our website, or added to any list of existing errata, under the Errata section of that title. Any existing errata can be viewed by selecting your title from `http://www.packtpub.com/support`.

Piracy

Piracy of copyright material on the Internet is an ongoing problem across all media. At Packt, we take the protection of our copyright and licenses very seriously. If you come across any illegal copies of our works, in any form, on the Internet, please provide us with the location address or website name immediately so that we can pursue a remedy.

Please contact us at `copyright@packtpub.com` with a link to the suspected pirated material.

We appreciate your help in protecting our authors, and our ability to bring you valuable content.

Questions

You can contact us at `questions@packtpub.com` if you are having a problem with any aspect of the book, and we will do our best to address it.

1
Getting to know haXe

Entering the haXe World.
In this chapter you will discover haXe's world and enter it. You'll install haXe and write your first program.

This is our first chapter and you will soon be taking your first steps with haXe. However, before you get into action, let's introduce you to haXe and set up your working environment.

In this chapter, you will:

- ◆ Install haXe
- ◆ Choose a code editor based on our requirements
- ◆ Write and run your first program
- ◆ Write a program interacting with the user

Seems like a long list? Don't be afraid, you will make it!

Installing haXe

Enough talking, let's install haXe! You will see how easy it is.

Two ways to install: The installer and sources compilation

You should know that there are two ways to install haXe, which are as follows:

1. Using the installer: An executable that will automatically install haXe for you.

2. Compiling from sources using the code repository located at the following URL:

   `http://code.google.com/p/haxe`

One important thing to note is that haXe can be installed on on Windows, Linux, and MacOSX. This way, you don't have to worry about your operating system and can continue working in your environment.

Installing on Windows

Installing haXe on Windows is pretty easy, but there are some caveats that we should avoid.

So, carry out the following steps:

1. Go to `http://www.haxe.org`.
2. Click on the **Download** link.
3. There, you will find a link to download the Windows version of the installer. It comes as an executable file.
4. Run the executable.

Note that if you're working on Windows Vista or Windows 7, you will need to run the executable as Administrator. You can do so by right-clicking on the installer while holding the *Shift* key down and then clicking on **Run as Administrator**.

Installing on MacOSX

Installing haXe on MacOSX is very straightforward. Carry out the following steps:

1. Go to `http://www.haxe.org`.
2. Click on the **Download** link.
3. There, locate and click on the link to download the **OSX Universal Installer**.
4. The installer comes as a DMG image, if it's not automatically mounted; mount it by double-clicking on it.
5. Go to where the DMG image is mounted and run the installer.

That's it! You have haXe installed on MacOSX!

Installing on Linux

Some distributions have haXe in their repositories, so you may install it from your distribution's repository if it's available.

Alternatively, you can use the Linux Installer to install haXe; it does work on many distributions. Carry out the following steps to install haXe on Linux:

1. Go to `http://www.haxe.org`.

2. Click on the **Downloads** link.

3. Find the link to download the Linux version of the installer.

4. Uncompress the file by using the `tar -zxf hxinst-linux.tgz` command.

5. Add execution rights on the installer by using the `chmod +x hxinst-linux` command.

6. Run the installer with administration rights either by using the `sudo -s` command or the `su -` command, and then running `./hxinst-linux`.

Now, you should have haXe installed on your Linux machine.

Installing nightly builds

If you need features that are not in the latest release, you can use the nightly builds to easily have access to binaries of what is in the repository without the need of compiling it on your own.

You will be able to find them on the haXe website's **Download** page for your operating system.

Note that the nightly builds do not come with an installer and therefore, you are advised to first install using the installer, so that it sets up all environment variables and then replaces installed files by the ones from the nightly builds archive.

On MacOSX and Linux machines, you should find them in `/usr/lib/haxe`, while on Windows, they should be in `c:\haxe`.

Verifying your installation

You can verify that haXe is correctly installed by opening a terminal and running the `haxe` command; if haXe is correctly installed, then you should get the help message.

You can also test that Neko is correctly installed by running the `neko` command. You should again get the help message.

Choosing an editor

There are not many editors for haXe, but still there are some that you should know of. Although I do suggest that you look at these because they can help you increase productivity. I do think that it's also important in the beginning to use the haXe compiler (that is, the `haxe` command) on your own to understand how it works and how it is used. You'll get more and more comfortable as you go through the examples.

FlashDevelop 3

The FlashDevelop IDE supports haXe projects. This is certainly the most advanced haXe code editor on Windows at the time of writing and also, it is an open source software.

FlashDevelop supports auto-completion, project management, syntax highlighting, and compilation rights from the IDE.

You can download FlashDevelop for free from `http://www.flashdevelop.org`. If you want to have a quick look at it before trying it, the following screenshot shows how it looks:

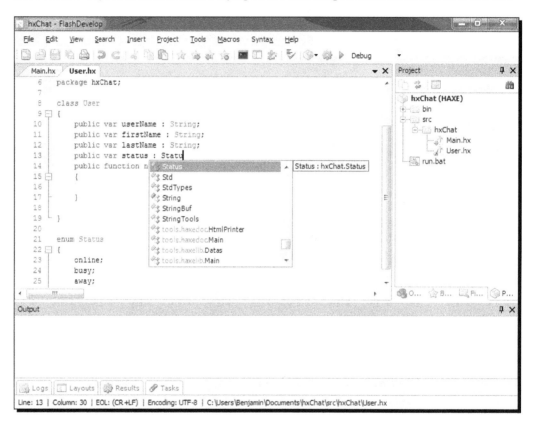

The TextMate bundle

TextMate is an easy-to-extend text editor for MacOSX. It can be extended by installing "bundles". There's a bundle providing haXe auto-completion, syntax highlighting and compilation from TextMate at `http://github.com/freewizard/haxe2.tmbundle`. You simply have to download the bundle as a ZIP file and rename it with the `.tmbundle` extension. Once this is done, double-click it. If you already have TextMate installed, the plugin should get installed.

The following screenshot shows what it looks like with the haXe bundle:

VIM

There are several scripts that you can install to add support for haXe in VIM. Many of these are collected at `http://github.com/MarcWeber/vim-haxe`. With those scripts, you get syntax highlighting and auto-completion. Although VIM is generally used by people using Linux, it can be used on Windows and MacOSX. This way, one can have the same tools across multiple platforms.

Writing your first program

So, you've installed haXe and got some advice in case you need help. Now is the time to get into action by writing your first program: and as usual, it will be a **Hello World**!

Time for action – Writing a Hello World

Let's create an application that will simply display the "Hello World" message. We will use only cross-platform code and will compile it to neko to begin.

1. Copy the following code in a file named Main.hx

```
class Main
{
    public static function main()
    {
        trace("Hello World");
    }
}
```

Downloading the example code for this book

You can download the example code files for all Packt books you have purchased from your account at http://www.PacktPub.com. If you purchased this book elsewhere, you can visit http://www.PacktPub.com/support and register to have the files e-mailed directly to you.

2. Open a terminal; go to the directory where you saved Main.hx and type the haxe -main Main -neko helloworld.n command.

3. Type this command: neko helloworld.n.

4. You will see the following output:

   Main.hx:5:Hello World

What just happened?

As you've guessed, the program just wrote "Main.hx:5:Hello World" in our terminal and ended.

- **The code**: In our code we declare a class named Main, which has a public and static function main. The method trace is a method that allows one to debug an application by printing a message along with the file's name and line number of the call. If you don't really understand what classes are, don't worry, we are going to explain it to you soon.

- **The compilation**: The command in the second step compiles the haXe code to neko. Notice that the -main switch that's followed by the name of the class containing the function has to be executed when launching the program. This function has to be a static function named main that takes no parameters.

◆ **Running the neko code**: In the third step, we invoke the neko VM and tell it to execute the `helloworld.n` file.

A program with some interaction

Now that we've gone through the classic "Hello World", let's do something a bit more interesting; how about taking some parameters on the command line? If you're not familiar with commands, this is the usual way to take some information from the user without having to write an interactive program.

Time for action – Interacting with the user

Now, we're going to create an application that takes your name as a parameter, greets you, and displays the number of characters in your name.

1. Copy the following code in a file named `Main.hx`

```
class Main
{
  public function new()
  {
  }
  public static function main()
  {
   var name = neko.Sys.args()[0];
   trace("Hello " + name);
   trace("Your name is " + Std.string(name.length) + "
     characters long.");
  }
}
```

2. Open a terminal; go to the directory where you saved `Main.hx` and type the `haxe -main Main -neko characterCounter.n` command.

3. Type the command (this is an example with my first name):

```
neko characterCounter.n Benjamin
```

4. You will see the following output:

Main.hx:12: Hello Benjamin

Main.hx:13: Your name is 8 characters long.

What just happened?

The program read your name from the command line, greeted you by appending your name to "Hello", and displayed the number of characters that make up your name.

- **The code**: You already know the basics about the class and the main function. What is interesting to see here is how we get the arguments. When targeting neko, we can use the args function of neko.Sys. This function takes no parameters and returns an **Array** of **String**.

  As you can see, we can access an array's item by its index using the square-brackets notation. Here we are accessing the item at index 0 (arrays are 0-based, that means that the first item is always at index 0).

  Then, we use the trace function that you've already seen to display "Hello" followed by the name of the user. As you can see here, string concatenation is done by using the + operator. It is still quite important to note that there are classes such as StringBuf that can be used to achieve the same behavior, if you are focused on performances.

  You'll also notice that String has a variable named length that allows you to retrieve the number of characters in it.

  By the way, haXe is typed, and here we are using Std.string to convert the length of the string from Int to String. Std.string can be used to convert any value to a String. This is not mandatory here, as when using the + operator, if one of the two values is not an Int nor a Float, the operator will return a String. In this case, all operands will be considered as String.

- **The compilation**: Well, as you can see, there's absolutely nothing new in the compilation process. The only thing we've changed is the output file's name.

- **Running the neko code**: In the third step, we invoke the neko VM and tell it to execute the characterCounter.n file by passing it an argument: Benjamin.

- **Possible improvements**: Our program is quite simple, but if you've some experience with programming, you may have noticed one point where our program may encounter an exception: we are relying on the fact that the user will give us at least one argument, and we access it directly without verifying that it's really there. So, if the user gives us no argument, we will encounter an exception. There are two ways to handle that: either we verify how many arguments the user has given, or we can also try to catch exceptions. This is something that we will explain later.

Pop quiz – basic knowledge

1. It is possible to install haXe on:
    a. Windows
    b. MacOSX
    c. Linux
    d. Android
    e. iOS

2. What major version do we use nowadays?
    a. haXe 1
    b. haXe 2
    c. haXe 3
    d. haXe 4

3. The main function of a program has to be:
    a. static and named main
    b. public and named first
    c. public and static, and named first

4. The debugging function that prints some text is named:
    a. println
    b. print
    c. trace
    d. debug

Summary

In this chapter, we have seen how to carry out your first steps with haXe. In particular, we've seen how to install haXe and how to write haXe programs. We've also seen how you can interact with the user in the console.

Now, let's go to the second chapter in which we will learn about the basic syntax and how to do branching.

2
Basic Syntax and Branching

Basic constructs and making decisions.

In this chapter, we will learn about basic haXe constructs and pieces that make a program. We will also learn about branching (those are indeed constructs too), so that your program can make decisions and choose different paths according to conditions.

In fact, this chapter is one of the most important to get you started because it will teach you how to tell a haXe program what to do.

In this second chapter, we are going to learn quite a lot of things. The great thing is that after this chapter, you will have the knowledge to create programs that won't always do the same things. You will know about all haXe constructs too and therefore, should be able to have fun with haXe.

In this chapter, we will:

- ◆ Learn about modules, packages, and classes
- ◆ Learn about constants
- ◆ Talk about binary and unary operators
- ◆ Learn what blocks are and their particularities
- ◆ Learn about variables and scope
- ◆ Talk about how to access fields and call methods
- ◆ Learn about conditional branching
- ◆ Learn about loops
- ◆ Learn about functions

- ◆ Learn about exceptions and how to handle them
- ◆ Learn about anonymous objects
- ◆ Learn about local functions
- ◆ Write our first complex application: a fridge management application

Don't be afraid of the list! Although it may seem quite long, you will see that it's all pretty easy to understand. This chapter is a pretty important one, so take the time to go through it. In this chapter, you will see a lot of short examples of code. You should read them carefully, and you should be able to understand them without too many explanations.

Modules, packages, and classes

If you're familiar with **Object Oriented Programming (OOP)** languages, then there are chances that you at least know the words "packages" and "classes"; if that's not the case, don't panic, you are going to learn all of it here.

Packages

Packages are a convenient way of splitting code into groups. Doing so, allows one to have several classes with the same name in different packages. This can be really useful, as you may, for example support two scripting languages in an application and need to write an interpreter class for each one.

Packages are represented by folders under your source directory on your filesystem. Each package has a path, which is a string obtained by joining the folders' name with dots. So, for example, if your source folder is `/dev/myProject/src` and you have a folder `/dev/myProject/src/proj/dao`, you have a package whose path is `proj.da` (you also have a package "proj"). There's a special package that has an empty path; it is named the top-level package and is represented by your source folder.

Each part of a package name must always begin with a lower-case character.

Note that you may have multiple source folders. Each of them should be given to the compiler with the `-cp` flag, also, the current working directory is automatically added to the list of source folders.

If you have files colliding in different source folders, the ones from the latest included source folder will take precedence over (hide) the others. This can be interesting to know sometimes, as you may have the feeling that your changes to a file are not taken into account.

Modules

Modules are stored in packages. They are represented by files with the `.hx` extension in your filesystem. They indeed are the files that will contain your haXe code. Modules follow the same naming scheme as packages, except that the first character of their name must be in uppercase. That means, if you have a file named `Food.hx in /src/bo/`, then the full path of your module will be `bo.Food`.

Modules will contain all the types, which you will declare. That can be classes, typedefs, interfaces, and enums. We will only talk about classes at the moment.

Modules can contain a main type that has the same name as the module. Also, note that if a module is in a package that's not the top-level package, it must begin by the line `package package.path`.

Classes

Classes are the base of Object Oriented Programming, but since this is not a book about OOP, we'll just have a quick reminder: classes are a bit like a blueprint. When you create an object from a class (what we call "instantiate"), you make sure that this object will have all the fields (such as variables, functions, and properties) declared in the class (but not those that are static). The object will also be of the type declared by the class.

The first character of a class' name must be uppercase.

Accessing a class

A class that is a module's main type can be accessed by using its complete path (that is, its package's path concatenated with a dot and its name) or by using its name, if using it from the same package.

If you want to access a class that is not the module's main type, you must use the complete path to the module concatenated with a dot and the class' name, or, if you're in the same module, you can simply use the class name.

Note that the two precedent paragraphs are true for all kinds of types in haXe.

The following is a commented example:

```
package food; //We are in the food package

class Meat //Full path to access this class : food.Meat
{
    public var name : String; //All instances of Meat will have a
      variable name of type String
    public var size : Int;
}
```

```
class Fruit //Full path to access this class : food.Meat.Fruit
{
    public var name : String;
    public var vitamins : String;
}
```

Constants and its types

There are six types of constants in haXe. We will now take a look at all of them. Some of them are composed of several kinds of them.

Booleans

The first type of constants is one that is spread most across programming languages: Booleans. For your information, in haXe Booleans have the type `Bool`. The following are two expressions, which are Boolean constants:

1. `true`
2. `false`

That's both easy and important. By the way, in haXe Bool is indeed an Enum (if you don't know what this is, don't worry, we will learn about it later). This Enum has two values, and true and false are just reference to these values.

Booleans are generally used to represent the truthiness of things. For example, when one is presented with a checkbox in an interface, the "checked" property of the checkbox can be of type Bool.

Integers

This one is easy; you can use integers constants by simply writing their values, for example:

◆ `1234`
◆ `-456`

You can also use the hexadecimal notation by starting your value with `0x`:

◆ `0xF`
◆ `0xF0`

The first example has a value of 15 and the second one has a value of 240.

Note that in haXe, integers have the type `Int`.

Floats

Floats can be written using two different notations; let's take a look at both.

Base 10

You can write floats values directly in base 10, as follows:

- ◆ `0.72`
- ◆ `-0.45`
- ◆ `.50`
- ◆ `-.23`

As you can see, if the integral part of your float is 0, you can simply omit it.

Scientific notation

Floats can be written using the scientific notation too: this should be pretty familiar to you:

- ◆ `1e2`
- ◆ `1e-3`
- ◆ `-2e4`
- ◆ `-2e-4`

The first value here is 100 and, before you ask, yes it's a float here! The second one is 0.001 and as you've guessed, the third one is -20000 and the fourth one is -0.002.

Strings

Strings can be written by simply enclosing them between two double quotes (") or between two single quotes ('). So, the following are two examples:

1. `"Hello World!"`
2. `'Hello Reader!'`

Those are simple strings, but you may also need to separate some special characters; this can be done using the back-slash (\) character, as follows:

1. `"Hello \"somebody\"\"somebody\""`
2. `'This one has a line-break\nhere'`

Also, note that in haXe, strings can span across several lines, so you could also write:

```
"This one has a line-break

here"
```

This is something which does not necessary exist in all languages, but it can be really useful.

Regular expressions

You can also write regular expressions by beginning them with ~/, so for example:

◆   ~/[a-ZA-Z]+/

Note that regular expressions in haXe have the type EReg.

The following is an example of how you can test whether a regular expression matches a String:

```
class TesthaXe
{
    public static function main(): Void
    {
        var e = ~/^Hello.*/; //Creates an EReg matching any string
            beginning with Hello. var e = simply declares the variable
            and assign the value on the right to it.
        if(e.match("Hello Benjamin"))
        {
            neko.Lib.println("Matches");
        } else
        {
            neko.Lib.println("Does not match");
        }
    }
}
```

This code will print Matches. The following is the same example written in a slightly different way. Note how the regular expression is created:

```
class TesthaXe
{
    public static function main(): Void
    {
        var e = new EReg("^Hello.*",""); //Creates an EReg matching any
            string beginning with Hello
        if(e.match("Hello Benjamin"))
```

```
    {
      neko.Lib.println("Matches");
    } else
    {
      neko.Lib.println("Does not match");
    }
  }
}
```

This code does exactly the same thing and the created regular expression is exactly the same. Note that the EReg's constructor takes two strings as its parameters: the first one is the pattern of the regular expression, while the other one contains the options of the regular expression. Also, note that such options can be passed when creating an EReg using the first notation by passing them after the second slash. For example: ~/[aZ]/g.

The null value

The null value can be represented using the null keyword. Please note that in haXe, null is of type Unknown<0>, which means that the compiler doesn't know what its type is. That may seem a bit strange but it does make sense; indeed, because of that you will be able to use the null value in place of any type.

Also, because null can be used for any type, you may want, particularly when converting some user input or when writing libraries, to test against a null value to avoid runtime errors.

The following is an example:

```
class TesthaXe
{
  public static function main(): Void
  {
    var l = new List<String>();
    printLoweredString(l.first());
  }

  public static function printLoweredString(s : String)
  {
    neko.Lib.println(s.toLowerCase());
  }
}
```

As the list is empty, the call to first will return a null value. In `printLoweredString`, the call to `toLowerCase` on a null value cannot succeed and will result in an exception being thrown at runtime. You can avoid this, by using the following example:

```
class TesthaXe
{
    public static function main(): Void
    {
        var l = new List<String>();
        if(l.first() != null)
        {
            printLoweredString(l.first());
        }
    }

    public static function printLoweredString(s : String)
    {
        neko.Lib.println(s.toLowerCase());
    }
}
```

Depending on how you want your code to behave, you may want to write the test in the `printLoweredString` function.

Also, note that using the first function twice certainly does not optimize the process; it would certainly be better to store the result in a variable.

Flash9 and above

In Flash9 and above, it's not possible to assign null to variables that are of a type considered as `basic`. Those types include, for example, `Int` and `String`.

If you want to be able to assign null to such variables, you have to declare them using the `Null` type, for example:

```
var e : Null<Int>;
```

Binary and unary operators

Binary and unary operators are two very important concepts in programming because they can both respectively be used to manipulate data. So, let's start with binary operators.

Binary operators

There are several operators, some of which you may already be familiar with, and some that you may not know, even if you have some programming experience. So, take a look at see all of them!

Assigning values

There are several operators that can assign a value to an expression:

Operator	Explanation
e1 = e2	Assigns the value of e2 to the expression e1. It returns the value of e2;
+= -+ *= /= %= &= |= ^= <<= >>= >>>=	Assigns the value to the expression on the left after performing the operation (see before). For example, a += 5; is equivalent to a = a + 5;. It will return the new value of the expression on the left.

Comparison operators

There are several comparison operators, all of them returning either true or false.

Operator	Explanation
e1 == e2	Returns true if e1 and e2 are equal.
e1 != e2	Returns false if e1 and e2 are equal.
e1> e2 or e1 < e2 or e1 >=e2 or e1 >=e2	Returns true if the comparison is true.

Arithmetic operators

Here are haXe's arithmetic operators; beware of their return type!

Operator	Explanation	Return type
e1 + e2	Adds the value of e1 to the value of e2	Int if both e1 and e2 are Int. Float if both are Int or Float (only one needs to be Float), or else it returns String.
e1 - e2	Subtracts the value of e2 from the value of e1.	Int if both e1 and e2 are Int. Returns Float as soon as one is Float.
e1 * e2	Multiplies the value of e1 with the value of e2.	See return type of subtraction.
e1 / e2	Divides the value of e1 by the value of e2.	Always returns Float.
e1 % e2	Returns the modulo of the value of e1 by the value of e2.	See return type of subtraction.

Boolean operators

Boolean operators compare two Boolean values and return a Boolean:

Operator	Explanation
e1&& e2	Performs the logical AND operation between e1 and e2.
e1 || e2	Performs the logical OR operation between e1 and e2.

Bitwise operators

These operators compare two integers bit to bit and always return an Int:

Operator	Explanation
e1 | e2	Bitwise OR between the value of e1 and the value of e2.
e1& e2	Bitwise AND between the value of e1 and the value of e2.
e1 ^ e2	Bitwise XOR between the value of e1 and the value of e2.
e1>> e2	Performs an arithmetic right shift on the value of e1 by the value of e2.
e1<< e2	Performs an arithmetic left shift on the value of e1 by the value of e2.
e1>>> e2	Performs a logical right shift on the value of e1 by the value of e2.

Unary operators

There are a few unary operators in haXe and most of them are pretty easy to read. Here they are as follows:

Operator	Explanation
!e1	Inverse the value of e1, where e1 is a Bool.
-e1	Inverse the sign of e1, where e1 is an Int or a Float.
++e1 or --e1	Increases or decreases the value of e1 and returns the value. e1 should be an Int or a Float. (see example below)
e1++ or e1--	Increments or decrements the value of e1 and returns the old value of e1. e1 should be an Int or a Float. (see example below)
~e1	Returns the one's complement of the value of e1. Be warned that it will produce unpredictable results on Neko because Neko's integers are 31 bits instead of being 32 bits.

That's it! We've finished with operators. There are some subtleties, such as pre and post incrementing.

The following is an example of increments:

```
class TesthaXe
{

    public static function main()
    {
        var i : Int = 0;
        var j : Int = 0;
        trace(i++);
        trace(++j);
    }
}
```

This will output the following:

TesthaXe.hx:8: 0

TesthaXe.hx:9: 1

This is because with `i++`, the value of `i` is returned before incrementing it, while in `++j`, the value is incremented before returning it.

Blocks

Blocks are important things in haXe, as they can help you write things that might be complicated in some languages in an easy way. Blocks are delimited in the C-style by the { and } characters. What makes them special in haXe is that they have a value and a type. A block's value and type is those of the last expression of this block. Note that empty blocks are of Void type. This type is used to indicate that no value is going to be returned.

Here's an example on how that may ease writing in some cases:

```
public static function main() : Void
{
    var s : String;
    s = if (true)
        {
            "Vrai";
        } else
        {
            "Faux";
        }
    trace(s);
}
```

In this example, it will always trace `Vrai` (which is the French translation of "True"), but I think you get the idea. In most other languages, you would have to write something like:

```
public static function main() : Void
{
   var s : String;
   if(true)
      {
         s = "Vrai";
      } else
      {
         s = "Faux";
      }
   trace(s);
}
```

That's more typing and may well become less readable in complex cases. This can bring some sort of functional programming paradigm to haXe. In this example, the case is fairly simple and remains easy to understand in both cases, but in many complex cases you will learn to love haXe's blocks.

Variable declaration and scope

Understanding how variable declaration is done and its scope is very important.

Declaring a variable

You can declare a variable by using the `var` keyword followed by the name of the variable. There are two syntaxes to declare a variable: one is to declare variables at class level, and another one is to declare local variables in blocks of instructions (inside functions, for example).

At class level

The following is the syntax you can use to declare a variable at the class level:

```
[public|private] [static] var varName [: varType] [= someValue];
```

Note that if you don't specify `public` or `private`, all members will be private unless the class implements the `Public` interface.

Static variables are variables that will be stored directly inside the class and not inside the instance of the class (this does mean that there will be only one value for them in the whole program). A static variable can only be accessed through the class, not through its instances. By the way, unlike member variables, you have the option to set a value to static variables at declaration time.

Time for action – Declaring some fields

Now, imagine that we want to create a class named `Person`. Its instances should have a public name field, a private age field, and the class should have a static and public count field.

1. The first thing we can do is to write it in the following way:

```
class Person
{
    public var name : String; //This one is public
    var age : Int; //This one is private
    public static var count : Int = 0; //This one is static and
        initialized at 0
}
```

2. On the other hand, we can write it by implementing the `Public` interface, as follows:

```
class Person implements Public
{
    var name : String; //This one is public
    private var age : Int; //This one is private
    static var count : Int = 0; //And this one is public
}
```

What just happened?

These two solutions will result in exactly the same thing:

♦   **Without implementing Public**: When a class does not implement Public, all of its fields are private by default. That's why we have to explicitly write that the name and count properties are public.

♦   **When implementing Public**: On the other hand, when implementing Public, a class' fields are public by default. That's why we can simply omit the visibility of the name and count fields while we have to explicitly define that the age field is private.

In a block of instructions

The syntax to declare a local variable is slightly different:

```
var varName [: Type] [= varValue];
```

As you can see, declaring the type is not mandatory and you can initialize your variable (not depending on anything). The following is a small sample of code, so that you can see how it looks:

```
class Main
{
    public static function main()
    {
        var myNumber : Int = 15;
    }
}
```

You should know that a variable is available starting from the line where it is declared, until the block it's declared in is closed, and for all blocks inside it.

A variable can be declared several times, either in the same block or in different blocks, as follows:

```
class Main
{
    public static function main()
    {
        var myNumber : Int = 15;
        var myNumber = 2;
        trace(myNumber); //Traces 2
        {
            var myNumber : Int = 1;
            trace(myNumber); //Traces 1
        }
        trace(myNumber); //Traces 2
    }
}
```

As you can see, it is always the closer declaration that is taken into account. That is classical variable hiding. Local variables only live in the block they are defined in.

Field access and function calls

Accessing fields and calling methods in haXe is quite easy. All fields of an object (that is all functions that are variables of this object) are accessed by using the dot notation. So, if you want to access the name variable of an object named user you can do so in the following way:

```
user.name
```

Calling a function is really easy too, all you have to do is put parentheses after the function's name and eventually write all of your arguments inside the parentheses, separated by commas. Here's how to call a function named `sayHelloTo` of an object named `user`, taking two strings as parameters:

```
user.sayHelloTo("Mr", "Benjamin");
```

That's all! It's quite easy, really.

Constructing class instance

Constructing a class instance is done using the `new` keyword, as follows:

```
var user = new User("Benjamin");
```

In this example, we create an instance of the `User` class. Doing so calls the class' constructor. The class constructor is defined in the class as the public non-static new function. It may take any number of parameters. The following is an example of our `User` class:

```
class User
{
    public function new(title : String, name : String)
    {
        //Do things
    }
}
```

You can call the superclass's constructor by calling `super()` (with parameters if needed).

You can access the current class instance using the `this` keyword.

Conditional branching

Conditional branching is a very important part of programming because it will allow your program to behave differently depending on the context. So, let's talk about `if` and `switch`.

If

The `if` expression allows you to test an expression; If it returns `true` then the following expression will be executed. You may also use the `else` keyword, followed by an expression, which will be executed if the test returns `false`. Note that a block of code is an expression.

The following is the general syntax:

```
if (condition) exprExecutedIfTrue [else exprExecutedIfTestFalse]
```

Now, let's look at some examples:

```
if(age<18)
{
    trace("you are not an adult.");
} else
{
    trace("You are an adult");
}
```

I think it is obvious here what this block of code does. Notice that this code could have been written in the following way too:

```
if(age<18)
    trace("you are not an adult.");
else
    trace("You are an adult");
```

This can be interesting to know, as it can save some typing when the block has only one line. On the other hand, some people prefer always writing brackets, as it can be more readable.

Or, using what we've learned about blocks:

```
class TesthaXe
{
    public static function main(): Void
    {
        var age = 18;
        trace(
            if(age<18)
            {
                are not an adult.";
            }
            else
            {
                are an adult";
            }
        );
    }
}
```

So, in this example, the program will give the output: You are an adult.

Now, a simple example with `else if`:

```
if(age < 16)
{
    trace("You are young!")
} else if(age >= 16 && age < 18)
{
    trace("You are almost an adult")
} else
{
    trace("You are an adult");
}
```

OK, this is almost the same thing, but it gives you an overview of how you can use `else if`.

`If` instructions can also be contained one into another, as shown in the following example:

```
class TesthaXe
{

    public static function main()
    {
        var age = 18;
        var country = "France";
        if(country == "France")
        {
            if(age < 18)
            {
                neko.Lib.println("You do not have the right to drink
                    everything.");
            } else
            {
                neko.Lib.println("You can drink anything you want.");
            }
        } else if(country == "USA")
        {
            if(age < 18)
            {
                neko.Lib.println("You do not have the right to drink
                    everything.");
            } else
            {
                if(age < 21)
                {
                    neko.Lib.println("Depending on the state, you may or
                        may not drink what you want.");
```

```
        } else
        {
            neko.Lib.println("You can drink anything you want.");
        }
    }
}
}
}
```

The preceding program is an idea for something that could be interesting to young travelers. Depending on your age and the country you're in (because some drinks may be forbidden to people of different ages depending on the state), it tries to determine if you can drink anything you want or not.

Note that this program is not expected to be accurate nor is it perfectly written. Indeed, it's certainly the worst way to write this algorithm, but it is there only to demonstrate what you can do.

Switch

The `switch` construct allows you to test the equality of a value against other values. So, let's go to an example directly:

```
switch(title)
{
    case "Mr":
        trace('You are man');
    case 'Ms', 'Melle':
        trace('You are a woman');
    default:
        trace('I don\'t know if you are a man or a woman');
}
```

This block of code uses the title of somebody to tell if it's a man or a woman. As you can see, after the `switch` keyword and inside parentheses, there is the value to test against. Then, after `case`, there are one or several values to test for equality. If there are several values, they should be separated by commas.

Note that there is no `break` keyword needed in haXe, only one case is called and the program will continue executing directly at the end of the switch block when reaching the end of the case.

The `default` keyword is there to indicate the code to execute if no value matches.

Again, this example could have been written this way:

```
class TesthaXe
{
    public static function main(): Void
    {
        var title = "Mr";
        trace(
            switch(title)
            {
                case "Mr":
                    'You are man';
                case 'Ms', 'Melle':
                    'You are a woman';
                default:
                    'I don\'t know if you are a man or a woman';
            }
        );
    }
}
```

I know I'm repeating myself, but trust me, you'll come to love this way of writing things.

Loops

Loops are one of the basic constructs in a language. So, let's see the loops that haXe supports.

While

While is a loop that is executed as long as a condition is true. It has the following two syntaxes:

```
while(condition) exprToBeExecuted;
doexprToBeExecuted while(condition);
```

With the first syntax, the condition is tested before entering the loop. That means, if the condition is not true, exprToBeExecuted will never be executed.

With the second syntax, the condition is tested after the execution of exprToBeExecuted. This way, you are sure that exprToBeExecuted will be executed at least once. The following are two simple examples to help you understand how these syntaxes have to be used:

```
public static function main()
{
    var i : Int = 0;
```

```
    while(i< 18)
    {
        trace(i); //Will trace numbers from 0 to 17 included
        i++;
    }
}
```

The preceding code is for the first syntax, and now, the second syntax:

```
public static function main()
{
    var i : Int = 0;
    do
    {
        trace(i); //Will trace numbers from 0 to 17 included
        i++;
    } while(i< 18);
}
```

The following is the trace from it:

TesthaXe.hx:9: 00

TesthaXe.hx:9: 1

TesthaXe.hx:9: 2

TesthaXe.hx:9: 3

TesthaXe.hx:9: 4

TesthaXe.hx:9: 5

TesthaXe.hx:9: 6

TesthaXe.hx:9: 7

TesthaXe.hx:9: 8

TesthaXe.hx:9: 9

TesthaXe.hx:9: 10

TesthaXe.hx:9: 11

TesthaXe.hx:9: 12

TesthaXe.hx:9: 13

TesthaXe.hx:9: 14

TesthaXe.hx:9: 15

TesthaXe.hx:9: 16

TesthaXe.hx:9: 17

For

haXe has a `for` loop that only supports working on iterators. An iterator is an object that supports some methods defined in the iterator `typedef`. It holds several values and returns them one by one at each call of the next function. The following is an example of a `for` loop:

```
for(i in 0...10)
{
    trace(i); // Will trace numbers from 0 to 9
}
```

`0...10` is a special construct. The `...` operator takes two integers and returns an iterator that will return all integers from the first one (included) to the last one (excluded).

The following is the printed text if you do not trust me:

TesthaXe.hx:8: 0

TesthaXe.hx:8: 1

TesthaXe.hx:8: 2

TesthaXe.hx:8: 3

TesthaXe.hx:8: 4

TesthaXe.hx:8: 5

TesthaXe.hx:8: 6

TesthaXe.hx:8: 7

TesthaXe.hx:8: 8

TesthaXe.hx:8: 9

This construct is particularly useful to iterate over arrays and lists. That's something we will see when we discuss arrays and lists, but the following is an example of it:

```
class TesthaXe
{
    public static function main(): Void
    {
        var l = new List<String>();
        l.add("Hello");
        l.add("World");
        for(s in l)
        {
            neko.Lib.println(s);
        }
    }
}
```

This code will print `Hello` at first and then `World` because it will iterate over the elements of the l list.

Break and continue

`break` and `continue` are two keywords used inside loops.

Time for action – Using the break keyword

The `break` keyword allows one to exit a loop prematurely. Now, let's imagine that we have a loop that has 10 iterations, but we only want to go through the first eight ones.

Let's write a simple loop from 0 to 9 included. Note that we want to exit this loop as soon as we hit the 9th one.

```
for(i in 0...10)
{
    if(i==8)
    {
        break;
    }
    trace(i);
}
```

What just happened?

At the beginning of each loop, we test whether we are in the 9th one or not, if we are, then we exit the loop by executing break.

The result of this code will be:

TesthaXe.hx:12: 0

TesthaXe.hx:12: 1

TesthaXe.hx:12: 2

TesthaXe.hx:12: 3

TesthaXe.hx:12: 4

TesthaXe.hx:12: 5

TesthaXe.hx:12: 6

TesthaXe.hx:12: 7

Time for action – Using the continue keyword

Let's say that we want to display the number from 0 to 9 included, but not the number 8. We can use the `continue` keyword to do so, by directly going to the next iteration of our loop.

Let's write the following code that contains our loop, and a test done at each iteration to jump to the next iteration if needed:

```
for(i in 0...10)
{
    if(i==8)
    {
        continue;
    }
    trace(i);
}
```

What just happened?

In this *Time for Action*, we test if i is equal to 8, if it is, we simply go to the next iteration, therefore avoiding the printing of i.

This code will display the following:

TesthaXe.hx:12: 0

TesthaXe.hx:12: 1

TesthaXe.hx:12: 2

TesthaXe.hx:12: 3

TesthaXe.hx:12: 4

TesthaXe.hx:12: 5

TesthaXe.hx:12: 6

TesthaXe.hx:12: 7

TesthaXe.hx:12: 9

Return

The `return` keyword is used to exit from a function or to return a value from a function (and exit it).

```
function isAdult (age : Int) : Bool
{
    if(age < 18)
    {
        return false;
    }
    return true;
}
```

This is a function that should help you understand how to use the `return` keyword. It returns `false` if the age is inferior to 18, or else it returns `true`.

Exception handling

Exceptions are messages passed from the inner call of your program to the outer call (it is going through the stack from the most recent call to the older one). In haXe, any object can be thrown as an exception. Exception handling (that is intercepting those messages) is done with the help of the `try` and `catch` keywords.

```
try
{
    doSomething();
```

```
} catch (e : Int)
{
   //If do something throws an Int this block of code will be
     executed.
} catch (e : String)
{
   //If do something throws a String this block of code will be
     executed.
} catch (e : Dynamic)
{
   //If do something throws something else this block of code will be
     executed.
}
```

As you can see in this example, you can specify different types of exceptions to intercept and execute different blocks of code according to these types. The `Dynamic` type allows you to intercept any type of exception that hasn't been intercepted before. Mind the order in which you write your blocks, as they are evaluated from top to bottom.

A message that's not handled at any point in your program may cause the program to exit abruptly, so you should pay attention to these.

Anonymous objects

Anonymous objects are objects that you create on the fly using brackets. The following is an example:

```
{ age : 12, name : "Benjamin" };
```

This object, despite not being created from any class, is typed. Its type is: `{age :Int, name : String}`.

The following is an example that you can run:

```
class TesthaXe
{
   public static function main(): Void
   {
      var user = {name : "Benjamin", age:12};
      neko.Lib.println("User " + user.name + " is " + user.age + "
        years old.");
   }
}
```

This program will print `User Benjamin is 12 years old`.

Local functions

Local functions are functions without a name. (often named "anonymous functions") They are values and as such can be assigned to any variable. The following is an example:

```
public class User
{
    var sayHello : String->Void;

    public function new()
    {
        sayHello =    function(to : String)
                {
                    trace("Hello" + to);
                };
    }
}
```

Local functions can access any local variable declared in the same scope as static variables, but cannot access the `this` variable.

Local functions are typed. The local function in the preceding example is typed as `String->Void`. A function that takes a `String`, an `Int`, and returns a `String` would be typed as `String ->Int -> String`.

So, continuing the previous example, one could call the function in the following way:

```
public class User
{
    var sayHello : String->Void;

    public function new()
    {
        sayHello =    function(to : String)
                {
                    trace("Hello " + to);
                };
        sayHello("World"); //Call the sayHello function.
    }
}
```

Note that the `sayHello` method could be called from another method, but only after the value of the `sayHello` variable is set (that is, after assigning the function to the `sayHello` variable); otherwise, trying to call a null value always results in a runtime error.

Managing a fridge

This has been a pretty long chapter and we are now going to create something, which takes advantage of all that you have seen!

Time for action – Managing a fridge

We are going to create software to manage a fridge. We want to be able to add meals inside it, and to list what is in it. Ok, let's start!

1. Create a folder that is going to hold your project's files.

2. Create two folders inside it: a `src` folder and a `bin` folder.

3. In your `src` folder, create a `MyFridge` folder. This way, we now have a `MyFridge` package.

4. In the `MyFridge` package, create a `Fridge.hx` file with the following code inside it:

    ```
    package MyFridge;
    class Fridge
    {
        public static var meals = new List<Meals>();
    }
    ```

5. This way, our fridge will hold a list of meals inside it. We can make this variable static because we will only have one fridge.

6. Now, in the `MyFridge` package, create a file named `Meal.hx` and write the following code in it:

    ```
    package MyFridge;

    class Meal
    {
        public var name : String;

        public function new(f_name : String)
        {
            this.name = f_name;
        }
    }
    ```

7. We now have a class `Meal` and its instances will have a name.

8. We will now create a menu. In your `src` folder create a file named `MyFridge.hx`

and write the following code in it:

```
import neko.Lib;

class MyFridge
{
 public static function main() : Void
 {
  var choice;
  do
  {
   Lib.println("Main Menu");
   Lib.println("1) Add new meal");
   Lib.println("2) List meals in fridge");
   Lib.println("9) Exit");
   var choice = neko.io.File.stdin().readLine();
   switch(choice)
   {
    case "1":
    var nMeal = new Meal(neko.io.File.stdin().readLine()); //Create
      the meal and ask user its name
    MyFridge.Fridge.meals.add(nMeal);//Add the meal to list
    case "2":
    Lib.println("Meals in fridge:")
    for(meal in MyFridge.Fridge.meals)
    {
     Lib.println(meal.name);
    }
   }
  } while(choice != "9");

 }
}
```

9. Now, we have a fully functional menu and software that does what we want.

What just happened?

If you've read this chapter, you should be able to understand what you have been doing on your own. I'll just give you some hints on some lines.

- **Writing to the console**: Here, we are writing to the console by using the neko.Lib. println function. It takes a String as a parameter and prints it on a new line.

- **Storing a list**: In the Fridge class, we have a List of Meal. We haven't discussed the List class yet and you may be wondering what those < and > characters are. Don't worry, we will explain that later. Basically, it's just to tell the compiler that we will be storing objects of type Meal in the list.

- **Reading from the command line**: Reading from the command line is done using neko.io.File.stdin().readLine(). This is a method that returns a String. Handling input and output will be discussed in more depth later.

Have a go hero – Throw Exceptions to prevent crashes

Now, create a class with a function taking two integers as parameters. This function will divide the first integer by the second one. As dividing by 0 is not possible, you will test if the second integer is equal to 0. If it is, throw an exception.

Summary

We learned a lot in this chapter about syntax.

Specifically, we covered how to declare classes and variables. We also covered how to iterate on lists and arrays, and how things are organized in haXe.

Don't worry, things will get easier now that we are done with the basics of the language.

3
Being Cross-platform with haXe

Targeting different platforms with the same code-base.

This chapter is about how to target several platforms from the same haXe code – the thing that haXe is known for.

haXe allows us to target several platforms; so, you may want to take advantage of this feature to be able to use your applications or libraries on several platforms. Unfortunately, there are some drawbacks, but don't worry, we will go through them and see how to work around them.

In this chapter, we will:

- See what is cross-platform in the standard library
- Talk about platform-specific packages
- Learn about their specificities
- Learn about conditional compilation

So, not only are we going to talk about being cross-platform, but also about platform-specific things. So, if you're ready, let's get started!

What is cross-platform in the library

The standard library includes a lot of classes and methods, which you will need most of the time in a web application. So, let's have a look at the different features. What we call standard library is simply a set of objects, which is available when you install haXe.

Object storage

The standard library offers several structures in which you can store objects. In haXe, you will see that, compared to many other languages, there are not many structures to store objects. This choice has been made because developers should be able to do what they need to do with their objects instead of dealing with a lot of structures, which they have to cast all the time.

The basic structures are array, list, and hash. All of these have a different utility:

- Objects stored in an array can be directly accessed by using their index
- Objects in a list are linked together in an ordered way
- Objects in an hash are tied to what are called "keys", but instead of being an Int, keys are a String

There is also the IntHash structure that is a hash-table using Int values as keys.

These structures can be used seamlessly in all targets. This is also, why the hash only supports String as indexes: some platforms would require a complex class that would impair performances to support any kind of object as indexes.

The Std class

The Std class is a class that contains methods allowing you to do some basic tasks, such as parsing a Float or an Int from a String, transforming a Float to an Int, or obtaining a randomly generated number.

This class can be used on all targets without any problems.

The haxe package

The haxe package (notice the lower-case x) contains a lot of class-specific to haXe such as the haxe.Serializer class that allows one to serialize any object to the haXe serialization format or its twin class haxe.Unserializer that allows one to unserialize objects (that is "reconstruct" them).

This is basically a package offering extended cross-platform functionalities.

The classes in the haxe package can be used on all platforms most of the time.

The haxe.remoting package

This package also contains a `remoting` package that contains several classes allowing us to use the haXe remoting protocol. This protocol allows several programs supporting it to communicate easily. Some classes in this package are only available for certain targets because of their limitations. For example, a browser environment won't allow one to open a TCP socket, or Flash won't allow one to create a server.

Remoting will be discussed later, as it is a very interesting feature of haXe.

The haxe.rtti package

There's also the `rtti` package. **RTTI** means **Run Time Type Information**. A class can hold information about itself, such as what fields it contains and their declared types. This can be really interesting in some cases, such as, if you want to create automatically generated editors for some objects.

The haxe.Http class

The `haxe.Http` class is one you are certainly going to use quite often. It allows you to make HTTP requests and retrieve the answer pretty easily without having to deal with the HTTP protocol by yourself. If you don't know what HTTP is, then you should just know that it is the protocol used between web browsers and servers.

On a side-note, the ability to make HTTPS requests depends on the platform. For example, at the moment, Neko doesn't provide any way to make one, whereas it's not a problem at all on JS because this functionality is provided by the browser.

Also, some methods in this class are only available on some platforms. That's why, if you are writing a cross-platform library or program, you should pay attention to what methods you can use on all the platforms you want to target.

You should note that on JS, the `haxe.Http` class uses `HttpRequest` objects and as such, they suffer from security restrictions, the most important one being the same-domain policy. This is something that you should keep in mind, when thinking about your solution's architecture.

You can make a simple synchronous request by writing the following:

```
var answer = Http.requestUrl("http://www.benjamindasnois.com");
```

It is also possible to make some asynchronous requests as follows:

```
var myRequest = new Http("http://www.benjamindasnois.com");
myRequest.onData = function (d : String)
                {
                    Lib.println(d);
                }
myRequest.request(false);
```

This method also allows you to get more information about the answer, such as the headers and the return code.

The following is an example displaying the answer's headers :

```
import haxe.Http;
#if neko
import neko.Lib;
#elseif php
import php.Lib;
#end

class Main
{

  static function main()
  {
    var myRequest = new Http("http://www.benjamindasnois.com");
    myRequest.onData = function (d : String)
    {
     for (k in myRequest.responseHeaders.keys())
     {
      Lib.println(k + " : " + myRequest.responseHeaders.get(k));
     }
    };
    myRequest.request(false);
  }

}
```

The following is what it displays:

```
X-Cache : MISS from rack1.tumblr.com

X-Cache-Lookup : MISS from rack1.tumblr.com:80

Via : 1.0 rack1.tumblr.com:80 (squid/2.6.STABLE6)

P3P : CP="ALL ADM DEV PSAi COM OUR OTRo STP IND ONL"
```

```
Set-Cookie : tmgioct=h6NSbuBBgVV2IH3qzPEPPQLg; expires=Thu, 02-Jul-2020
23:30:11
 GMT; path=/; httponly
ETag : f85901c583a154f897ba718048d779ef
Link : <http://assets.tumblr.com/images/default_avatar_16.gif>; rel=icon
Vary : Accept-Encoding
Content-Type : text/html; charset=UTF-8
Content-Length : 30091
Server : Apache/2.2.3 (Red Hat)
Date : Mon, 05 Jul 2010 23:31:10 GMT
X-Tumblr-Usec : D=78076
X-Tumblr-User : pignoufou
X-Cache-Auto : hit
Connection : close
```

Regular expressions and XML handling

haXe offers a cross-platform API for regular expressions and XML that can be used on most targets' target.

Regular expressions

The regular expression API is implemented as the EReg class. You can use this class on any platform to match a RegExp, split a string according to a RegExp, or do some replacement.

This class is available on all targets, but on Flash, it only starts from Flash 9.

The following is an example of a simple function that returns true or false depending on if a RegExp matches a string given as parameter:

```
public static function matchesHello(str : String) : Bool
{
    var helloRegExp = ~/.*hello.*/;
    return helloRegExp.match(str);
}
```

One can also replace what is matched by the RegExp and return this value. This one simply replaces the word "hello" with "bye", so it's a bit of an overkill to use a RegExp to do that, and you will find some more useful ways to use this possibility when making some real programs. Now, at least you will know how to do it:

```
public static function replaceHello(str : String) : String
{
    var helloRegExp = ~/hello/;
    helloRegExp.match(str);
    return helloRegExp.replace(str, "bye");
}
```

XML handling

The XML class is available on all platforms. It allows you to parse and emit XML the same way on many targets. Unfortunately, it is implemented using RegExp on most platforms, and therefore can become quite slow on big files. Such problems have already been raised on the JS targets, particularly on some browsers, but you should keep in mind that different browsers perform completely differently.

For example, on the Flash platform, this API is now using the internal Flash XML libraries, which results in some incompatibilities.

The following is an example of how to create a simple XML document:

```
<pages>
    <page id="page1"/>
    <page id="page2"/>
</pages>
```

Now, the haXe code to generate it:

```
var xmlDoc : Xml;
var xmlRoot : Xml;
xmlDoc = Xml.createDocument(); //Create the document
xmlRoot = Xml.createElement("pages"); //Create the root node
xmlDoc.addChild(xmlRoot); //Add the root node to the document

var page1 : Xml;
page1 = Xml.createElement("page"); //create the first page node
page1.set("id", "page1");
xmlRoot.addChild(page1); //Add it to the root node

var page2 : Xml;
page2 = Xml.createElement("page");
page2.set("id", "page2");
xmlRoot.addChild(page2);

trace(xmlDoc.toString()); //Print the generated XML
```

Input and output

Input and output are certainly the most important parts of an application; indeed, without them, an application is almost useless.

If you think about how the different targets supported by haXe work and how the user may interact with them, you will quickly come to the conclusion that they use different ways of interacting with the user, which are as follows:

- JavaScript in the browser uses the DOM
- Flash has its own API to draw on screen and handle events
- Neko uses the classic input/output streams (`stdin`, `stdout`, `stderr`) and so do PHP and C++

So, we have three different `main` interfaces: DOM, Flash, and classic streams.

The DOM interface

The implementation of the DOM interface is available in the `js` package. This interface is implemented through typedefs. Unfortunately, the API doesn't provide any way to abstract the differences between browsers and you will have to deal with them in most cases by yourself.

This API is simply telling the compiler what objects exist in the DOM environment; so, if you know how to manipulate the DOM in JavaScript, you will be able to manipulate it in haXe. The thing that you should know is that the document object can be accessed through `js.Lib.document`.

The `js` package is accessible only when compiling to JS.

The Flash interface

In a way that is similar to how the Flash is implemented in the `flash` and `flash9` packages, the `js` package implements the DOM interface. When reading this sentence, you may wonder why there are two packages. The reason is pretty simple, the Flash APIs pre and post Flash 9 are different.

You also have to pay attention to the fact that, when compiling to Flash 9, the `flash9` package is accessible through the `flashpath` and not through `flash9`.

Also, at the time of writing, the documentation for `flash` and `flash9` packages on `haxe.org` is almost non-existent; but, if you need some documentation, you can refer to the official documentation.

The standard input/output interface

The standard input/output interface refers to the three basic streams that exist on most systems, which are as follows:

1. `stdin` (most of the time the keyboard).
2. `stdout` (the standard output which is most of the time the console, or, when running as a web-application, the stream sent to the client).
3. `stderr` (the standard error output which is most of the time directed to the console or the log file).

Neko, PHP and C++ all make use of this kind of interface. Now, there are two pieces news for you: one good and one bad.

The bad one is that the API for each platform is located in a platform-specific package. So, for example, when targeting Neko, you will have to use the `neko` package, which is not available in PHP or C++.

The good news is that there is a workaround. Well, indeed, there are three. You just have to continue reading through this chapter and I'll tell you how to handle that.

Platform-specific packages

You've already understood that there are some platform-specific packages, let's have an overview of them.

JavaScript

The platform-specific package for JavaScript is the `js` package. It basically contains only `typedefs` representing the DOM and has a layout that's not comparable to any one of the other platform-specific package.

Flash

As we've already mentioned, Flash has two platform-specific packages: the first one is `flash` and it is used when targeting Flash up to Flash 8, or else, you use the `flash9` package (but access it by writing `flash`). Those packages contain definitions for the external classes that are natives in Flash. Their layouts are not comparable to any other platform-specific packages.

Neko

Neko has its own package named `neko`. It contains a lot of useful classes allowing for example, sockets communication, file-system access, console input and output, and threads management.

Its layout is comparable to the layouts of the C++ and PHP packages.

PHP

The `php` package is a PHP-specific package. It allows us to manipulate files, write, and read from the console and open sockets.

Its layout is comparable to the layouts of the C++ and Neko packages.

C++

C++ has its specific package named `cpp`. It allows one to access the filesystem, read, and write from the console and open sockets.

Its layout is comparable to the layouts of the `neko` and `php` packages.

Conditional compilation

haXe allows you to do conditional compilation. This means that some parts of the code can be compiled and others can be ignored depending on the flags you give to the compiler and depending on the platform you're targeting.

Conditional compilation instructions always begin with the `#if` instruction.

Conditional compilation depending on flags

You can define a flag on the command line by using the `-D` switch. So, to define the `myway` flag, you would use the following: `-D myway`.

Then, you use it in the following way:

```
#if myway
//Code here compiled only if myway is defined
#else
//Code here compiled in the other case
#end
```

There is also a not operator:

```
#if !myway
//Code here compiled only myway is not defined
#end
```

Conditional compilation depending on the target

Conditional compilation depending on the target basically works in the same way, except that the name of the target you are compiling to automatically gets set. So, you will have something like the following:

```
#if cpp
//C++ code
#elseif neko
//Neko code
#elseif php
//PHP code
#else
//Code for other targets
#end
```

By the way, did you notice the presence of #elseif in the code? It could prove to be pretty useful if you need to create a different implementation of the same feature depending on the platform.

The remap switch

The compiler has a remap switch that allows us to rename a package, for example, imagine the following code:

```
//Some previous code
myPack.Lib.println("Hello remapping!");
//Some code following
```

This would obviously not work because the Lib class is not in the myPack package. However, if you compile with the switch --remap myPack:neko when compiling to Neko, this will work. The reason is simple: anywhere you have used the package name myPack; the compiler will replace it with Neko, therefore using the correct package.

This can be used to make some cross-platform code.

On the other hand, it has a big draw-back: when you remap a package, all of the modules it contains are remapped. This actually means that you won't be able to use something that is platform-specific inside this package.

Coding cross-platform using imports

We've already seen the import keyword that allows us to import all the classes of a module. This keyword can be used to write some cross-platform code. Indeed, it is the preferred way to do so, when working with packages that have the same layout. It has the advantage of being easily readable and does not mean adding three lines every time you want to access a platform-specific package.

So, here's a simple example: imagine you want to target Neko and PHP and want to use the println method available in neko.Lib.println and php.Lib.println (these methods allow you to write a line of text on the stdout). As you can see here, regarding what we are going to use, the neko and php package have the same layout (indeed, they have the same layout for quite a lot of their classes). So, we can write the following code:

```
#if php
import php.Lib;
#elseif neko
import neko.Lib;
#end

class Main

{

    public static function main()

    {

        Lib.println("Hello World");

    }

}
```

In this example, we can use the php.Lib or neko.Lib class by simply using its name (Lib), as the good one is imported depending on the current compilation target. If we didn't do that, the code would have looked like the following:

```
class Main
{
    public static function main()
    {
        #if php
        php.Lib.println("Hello World");
        #elseif neko
        neko.Lib.println("Hello World");
        #endif

    }

}
```

As you can see, this is pretty difficult to read although here we have almost no logic and only one instruction.

Time for action – Welcoming the user on Neko & PHP

We are going to write a simple program that asks the user their name and prints a little welcome message along with the date. This program should work with the same codebase on Neko and PHP.

The following are the steps you should follow to write this program:

1. Identify what classes you will need to print text and read from the keyboard.

2. Identify what classes are in a platform-specific package.

3. Add imports for those classes.

4. Run and test.

5. You should get the following output:

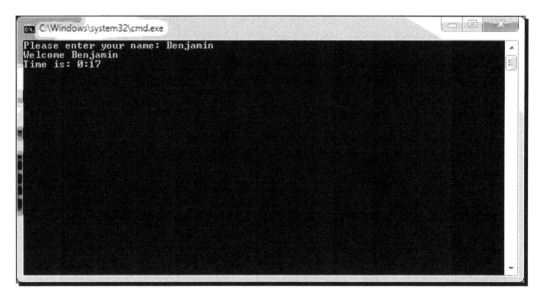

The following is the final code you should have produced:

```
#if neko
import neko.Lib;
import neko.io.File;
#elseif php
import php.Lib;
```

```
import php.io.File;
#end

class Main
{

    static function main()
    {
        //Print a prompt
        Lib.print("Please enter your name: ");
        //Read the answer
        var name = File.stdin().readLine();
        //Print the welcome message
        Lib.println("Welcome " + name);
        //Store the date
        var date = Date.now();
        //Concatenate a message with the two elements from the date
          object
        Lib.println("Time is: " + Std.string(date.getHours()) + ":" +
          Std.string(date.getMinutes()));
    }

}
```

What just happened?

I'm pretty sure that with the commented code, you do understand what's going on, but let's clarify each step we have asked you to think about:

◆ Needed classes

    ❑ To write to the console, we will use the `neko.Lib` class

    ❑ To read from the keyboard, we will use the `neko.io.File` class

    ❑ To know the date and time, we will use the `Date` class

◆ Identifying platform-specific classes

    ❑ The `neko.Lib` and `neko.io.File` classes obviously are platform-specific; their corresponding classes for PHP respectively are `php.Lib` and `php.io.File`

    ❑ The `Date` class is platform-independent and therefore, we won't need to do anything special with it

♦ Imports

We just have a section to do the good important according to the target platform:

```
#if neko
import neko.Lib;
import neko.io.File;
#elseif php
import php.Lib;
import php.io.File;
#end
```

This one is pretty short, but sometimes you may have many of those classes.

Pop quiz – Writing cross-platform code

1. What is the main drawback of using conditional compilation directly inside your code?

   a. It is more difficult to read

   b. It takes more time to compile

   c. It is less efficient at runtime

   d. It simply doesn't work

2. How does one access the `flash9` package when targeting Flash9+?

   a. Use the `–remap flash9:flash` switch

   b. Simply access it by writing flash9

   c. Access it by writing flash; the compiler knows what to do

   d. Use an `import` at the beginning of the file

Have a go hero – Handle XML

Now, let's sum-up all we've done and more particularly the XML part.

Imagine you want to create a tool, which allows you to create pages. Each page will be composed of one or several layers and each layer will have an ID.

You want to save and load a page in an XML file that will look like the following:

```
<page name="My First Page">
   <layer id="layer1">
      [content]
   </layer>
   <layer id="layer2">
```

```
      [content]
   </layer>
</page>
```

For the sake of this example, we will not generate the content parts.

Time for action – Reading from the XML file

We are going to create a function to read from an XML file. So, let's proceed step by step.

1. First, create the `Layer` class as follows:

```
class Layer
{
    public var id : String;

    public function new()
    {}
}
```

2. Now create the `Page` class as follows:

```
class Page
{
    public var name : String;
    public var layers : List<Layer>;

    public function new()
    {
    }
}
```

3. Now, let's create a function to create a page from an XML file. Add the following function to the `Page` class:

```
public static function fromXMLFile(path : String) : Page
{
    var nPage = new Page();
    var xmlDoc = Xml.parse(neko.io.File.read(path, false).
      readAll().toString());
    nPage.name = xmlDoc.firstElement().get("name");

    return nPage;
}
```

4. As you can see, it is not yet complete. We have to parse a layer from the XML file, so let's do it now. Add the following function in the `Layer` class:

```
public static function fromXMLNode(node : Xml)
{
    var nLayer : Layer;
    nLayer = new Layer();
    nLayer.id = node.get("id");

    return nLayer;
}
```

5. Now, in the `fromXMLFile` function, let's add some code to iterate over the nodes named `layers`, and parse them using the `fromXMLNode` function:

```
public static function fromXMLFile(path : String) : Page
{
    var nPage = new Page();
    var xmlDoc = Xml.parse(neko.io.File.read
      (path, false).readAll().toString());
    nPage.name = xmlDoc.firstElement().get("name");
    for(l in xmlDoc.firstElement().elementsNamed("layer"))
    {
        nPage.layers.add(Layer.fromXMLNode(l));
    }
    return nPage;
}
```

What just happened?

As you see, we are simply expecting our document to respect the structure that we have defined; therefore, it was pretty easy to parse our XML file.

Time for action – Writing to an XML file

1. We want to be able to write an XML file. To write the XML file, we will follow the same idea. Add the following function in the `Layer` class:

```
public function toXMLNode() : Xml
{
    var nXml = Xml.createElement("layer");
    nXml.set("id", this.id);
    return nXml;
}
```

2. Now, add the following code in the Page class:

```
public function toXMLFile(path : String)
{
   var xmlDoc = Xml.createDocument();
   var pageNode = Xml.createElement("page");
   pageNode.set("name", this.name);
   xmlDoc.addChild(pageNode);

   for(l in layers)
   {
      pageNode.addChild(l.toXMLNode());
   }

   neko.io.File.write(path, false).writeString(xmlDoc.toString());
}
```

You can now save a page and all its layers by calling toXMLFile.

What just happened?

We have created a simple of the function in order to be able to save our page as an XML file by calling toXMLFile.

Testing our sample

The following is a sample main function if you want to try this code. It may also help you to understand how to use it:

```
public static function main(): Void
{
   trace('Hello World');
   trace(Page.fromXMLFile("/Users/benjamin/example.xml"));
   trace(Page.fromXMLFile("/Users/benjamin/example.xml"));

   var p = new Page();
   p.name = "Page de test";

   var l1 = new Layer();
   l1.id="l1";
   var l2 = new Layer();
   l2.id-"l2";

   p.layers.add(l1);
   p.layers.add(l2);

   p.toXMLFile("/Users/benjamin/page1.xml");
}
```

Making it cross-platform

This code works on the Neko target. Using what we've learned about using imports to make code cross-platform, you can make this code work on PHP very easily. That's something you should try on your own to learn!

Summary

In this chapter, we've learned about how to do some cross-platform programming with haXe.

Specifically, we covered what is in the Standard Library, how to use conditional compilation and other ways to write cross-platform code, and how to handle XML files.

Now, let's move on to our next chapter in which we will talk about the typing system!

4
Understanding Types

Understanding the type system.

In this chapter, you will learn about the typing system. haXe is a strongly typed language but provides quite a lot of features such as type inference and Dynamic objects.

haXe has a typing system, which offers a lot of features. Understanding these features is very important to write and debug your programs. It will also help you make the most out of haXe.

In this chapter, we will:

- ◆ Talk about explicitly typed variables
- ◆ Talk about function's type.
- ◆ Learn what type inference is
- ◆ Learn how to cast variables
- ◆ Learn about type parameters
- ◆ See what type parameters are used for
- ◆ How you can use them with already created types
- ◆ How you can create a type that makes use of them
- ◆ Create an example

All of these points are fairly easy to understand and we are going to illustrate them in several exercises.

Explicitly typed variables

Variables are explicitly typed if you write their type while declaring them. This is what we have seen so far; and this is done in the following way:

```
var myVar : TypeOfMyVariable
```

This way, you tell the type of your variable to the compiler.

Static typing

In haXe, once a variable has been declared and its type is known, it is not possible to assign a value of another type to it. Note however that the compiler allows you to redeclare a variable with the same name and another type. So, the following code compiles:

```
class Main
{
    public static function main()
    {
        var e : String;
        e = "String";
        var e : Int;
        e = 12;
    }
}
```

However, although this code compiles, you should not be doing this because it might be confusing to other developers or even to you as well, if you have to read your code several days later.

Therefore, to keep things simple, once a variable is typed, its type cannot be changed, and only values of this type can be assigned to it. So, the following wouldn't work:

```
class Main
{
    public static function main()
    {
        var e : String;
        e = "Test";
        e = 12;
    }
}
```

This is because 12 is of type Int and not of type String.

Also, note that if you try to read from a variable without having assigned a value to it, the compiler will issue a warning saying that the variable has not been initialized.

Values with several types

If you are experienced in OOP, you may wonder how this is possible, but chances are that you already know about it.

Defining a type

In haXe, every time you write a class, an enum, an interface, or a typedef, you are defining a new type. This type has the same path (the same name) as the class, enum, interface, or typedef you are writing.

Inheritance

In haXe, a class can extend another class. In such a case, not only does it have all of the fields (that is properties and functions) of all its parent classes, but also all the types that its parent classes have (in addition to its own type).

What that means is that, for example, when a function wants a parameter of type A, if B extends A, you can pass an instance of B to your function. This is illustrated in the following code:

```
class Main
{
   public static function main()
   {
      var human : HumanBeing;
      human = new HumanBeing("Benjamin");
      congratulate(human);
   }

   public static function congratulate(lt : LivingThing)
   {
      trace("Congrats " + lt.name);
   }
}

class LivingThing
{
   public var name : String;

   public function new()
```

```
        {
            name = "";
        }
    }

    class HumanBeing extends LivingThing
    {
        public function new(name : String)
        {
            super();
            this.name = name;
        }
    }
```

Note how we can pass an instance of HumanBeing where a variable of type LivingThing is expected?

Multi-inheritance

haXe does not support any kind of multi-inheritance. Although this has already been discussed on the haXe mailing list, this proposal has been rejected until now in order to keep the language pretty simple, because it's a generally misused concept and also because haXe has to target several languages and there are not many languages that allow the use of multi-inheritance. Note that it does not necessarily mean that haXe would not be able to simulate it in those languages, but it would certainly have a severe impact on performance.

Implementing an interface

There's another way to have values with several types: using interfaces.

Interfaces are only a description of what a class should implement to have a certain type. In this case, instead of using the extends keyword, we will use the implements keyword. In addition, each class implementing an interface needs to have its own code for the method defined.

Let's see an example by extending the LivingThing and the HumanBeing example. We all know that some living things in our world are capable of making noise, let's see how we can describe that with an interface:

```
    interface INoiseAble
    {
        public function makeNoise() : Void;
    }
```

This is a pretty simple example and the interface could for sure be more complex. Now, we all know that the `HumanBeing` is able to make noise; so, let's write it:

```
class HumanBeing extends LivingThing, implements INoiseAble
{
    public function new(name : String)
    {
        super();
        this.name = name;
    }
}
```

Notice the comma before the implements keyword. It is important not to forget it, otherwise you may be wondering why the compiler tells you that there is an "unexpected implements" for a long time.

If you try to compile the code now, you will get an error saying: "Field `makeNoise` needed by `INoiseAble` is missing". Well, it is pretty self-explanatory: it simply means that we forgot to write the code for our `HumanBeing` to make some noise:

```
class HumanBeing extends LivingThing, implements INoiseAble
{
    public function new(name : String)
    {
        super();
        this.name = name;
    }

    public function makeNoise() : Void
    {
        trace("Hello.");
    }
}
```

Now, you can compile the code without any error. Now, let's modify our `Main` class, so that it can take any `INoiseAble` value and make it make some noise:

```
class Main
{
    public static function main()
    {
        var human : HumanBeing;
        human = new HumanBeing("Benjamin");
        makeNoiseWith(human);
    }
```

```
public static function congratulate(lt : LivingThing)
{
    trace("Congrats " + lt.name);
}

public static function makeNoiseWith(val : INoiseAble)
{
    val.makeNoise();
}
}
```

Now you can compile without any problems. We are able to pass the human variable as an argument to makeNoiseWith because the HumanBeing class implements INoiseAble; therefore, the value of human is also of type INoiseAble. This is called "polymorphism".

Note that interfaces cannot be extended, but an interface can "implement" another interface.

Representing a blog article

Many people do have a blog nowadays, as do many companies. They sometimes need something special and want a developer to write software for their own use.

Ready? It is time for action!

Time for action – Representing different types of articles

Now, imagine that the company you work for wants a blog with different types of articles—text-based articles and image-based articles. What they want is simple: a text-based article that is made of a String, and an image-based article that stores the URL of the image. All types of articles need to have a title.

At first, let's write the Article class. This one will define what all articles have.

```
class Article
{
    public var title : String;
}
```

Notice that we did not create a constructor for this class: an article has to be either text-based or image-based in this example, being able to construct an instance of the Article class would be nonsense.

We want text-based and image-based articles to be able to generate some HTML code, but each one will need to do it in its own way. To make it usable by a calling function, we will define an `IHTMLGenerator` interface, as follows:

```
interface IHTMLGenerator
{
   public function generateHTML() : String;
}
```

1. Now let's write what a text-based article is:

```
class TextArticle extends Article, implements IHTMLGenerator
{
   public var text : String;

   public function new(text : String)
   {
      this.text = text;
   }

   public function generateHTML() : String
   {
      returnStringTools.htmlEscape(text);
   }
}
```

2. Now, let's define what an image-based article is:

```
class ImageArticle extends Article, implements IHTMLGenerator
{
   public var imageUrl : String;

   public function new(url : String)
   {
      this.imageUrl = url;
   }

   public function generateHTML() : String
   {
      return '<imgsrc="' + this.imageUrl +
        '" alt=' + this.title + '/>';
   }
}
```

3. Finally, in our `Main` class, we will add two methods: one that displays the title of an article and one that outputs its HTML code:

```
class Main

{
   public static function main()
   {
      var imgArt : ImageArticle;
      imgArt = new ImageArticle
      ("http://www.someuninterestingblog.unexistingtld/someimage.
      png");
      imgArt.title = "Some unexisting image";
      var textArt : TextArticle;
      textArt = new TextArticle("This is an interesting text");
      textArt.title =  "Some interesting article";

      displayArticleTitle(imgArt);
      outputHTMLCode(imgArt);
      displayArticleTitle(textArt);
      outputHTMLCode(textArt);
   }
   public static function displayArticleTitle(art : Article)
   {
      trace(art.title);
   }
   public static function outputHTMLCode
      (generator : IHTMLGenerator)

   {
      trace(generator.generateHTML());
   }
}
```

4. Now, you can compile and run your code! You should get the following output:

```
Main.hx:20: Some unexisting image
Main.hx:25: <img src="http://www.someuninterestingblog.
unexistingtld/someimage.png"/>
Main.hx:20: Some uninteresting article
Main.hx:25: This is an uninteresting text
```

Function's type

Functions are typed too. That's good for two reasons: you can pass a function as a parameter to another function, and you can also store typed functions in a variable!

Expressing a function's type

All functions in haXe are typed, so for example, when you write:

```
public function outputString(st : String) : Void;
```

we know that the `outputString` function takes one parameter of type `String` and returns `Void` (that actually means that it does not return any object). This is represented as the following type:

```
String->Void
```

Now, imagine the following function:

```
public function sumAndCeil(a : Float, b : Int) : Int
```

Its type is:

```
Float->Int->Int
```

Ok, this was the easy part.

Functions using functions

As mentioned earlier, a function can be given as an argument to another function. That also means that a function can take a function as an argument. This is useful, for example, to apply filters on lists or arrays. There's such a case in the standard library: `List.filter`. I will simplify things a little bit by saying that this method, on a list of String, could be declared as follows:

```
public function filter(f : String->Bool) : List<String>
```

As you may have guessed, this function takes a function as a parameter, passes each element of the list to it, if the function returns true, then it adds the element to a list that it returns.

The type of this function is:

```
(String->Bool)->List<String>
```

So, when you want to write the type of a function that uses functions, you simply need to put parentheses around the function's type.

Functions can also return a function; in this case, you simply need to put parentheses after the last arrow of the type:

```
public function takesStringReturnsFunction(s : String) : String->Bool
```

This function has the type:

```
String->(String->Bool)
```

It takes a String and returns a function that takes a String and returns a Bool. Calling the returned function would be as simple as writing:

```
takesStringReturnsFunction("Hello")("World");
```

Dynamic functions

You can mark a function as being "dynamic". When you do so, you will be able to replace a function with another one (with the limit that it should be of the same type).

Being able to do that may allow you to change the behavior of a particular instance of a class. This is a powerful feature, but you should remember that, on the other hand, it can be costly in terms of performances on some platforms.

The following is a simple example:

```
class TestFunction
{
    public function new()
    {
    }

    public static function main(): Void
    {
        var m = new TestFunction();
        m.saySomething();
        m.saySomething = function () {
            trace("Hi.");
        };
        m.saySomething();
    }

    public dynamic function saySomething()
    {
        trace("Hello.");
    }
}
```

If you run the preceding code, you will see that the first trace will be "Hello." while the other one will be "Hi.". This actually proves that we have been dynamically changing the behavior of our instance of TestFunction. Now, let's see what happens when we have two instances:

```
class TestFunction
{
    public function new()
    {
    }

    public static function main(): Void
    {
        var m = new TestFunction();
        var n = new TestFunction();
        m.saySomething();
        m.saySomething = function () {
            trace("Hi.");
        };
        m.saySomething();
        n.saySomething();
    }

    public dynamic function saySomething()
    {
        trace("Hello.");
    }
}
```

As you can see when running the code, the last trace will be "Hello.", proving that the modification of the function takes place at the instance level.

Note that the dynamic keyword can also be applied to static functions as illustrated by the following example:

```
class TestFunction
{
    public function new()
    {
    }

    public static function main(): Void
    {
        var m = new TestFunction();
        var n = new TestFunction();
        TestFunction.saySomething();
        TestFunction.saySomething = function () {
```

```
        trace("Hi.");
    };
    TestFunction.saySomething();
}

public static dynamic function saySomething()
{
    trace("Hello.");
}
}
```

As you can see, this compiles and works as expected. Note however that overriding a dynamic function is impossible. It is also impossible to use super in a dynamic function.

Anonymous objects

Anonymous objects are objects that are of an unnamed type ("Anonymous Type"). They are made of a list of fields and their associated values. For example, here is how we can create one:

```
var obj = {id : 1, name : "Benjamin"};
```

Although the type of this object doesn't have a name, obj is still fully typed as {id :Int, name : String}. This is an anonymous type.

This is sometimes useful, if there is a type that you are not going to use a lot of time. By the way, this variable could be declared this way:

```
var obj : {id : Int, name : String};
```

Duck typing

Duck typing makes reference to an old cliché of "if it walks and talks like a duck, then it's a duck". In fact, we can use anonymous types to say that we want something that has at least some fields.

The following is an example:

```
class TestAnonymous
{
    public var name : String;
    public function new(name : String)
    {
        this.name = name;
    }
```

```
public static function main(): Void
{
    var m;
    sayHello(new TestAnonymous("Benjamin"));
}

public static function sayHello(obj : {name : String})
{
    trace("Hello " + obj.name);
}
}
```

In this example, the sayHello function wants an object as a parameter that will have a field name of type String. The TestAnonymous instance satisfies this constraint and therefore, it can be given as a parameter to the sayHello function.

This can be particularly helpful when writing helper functions, in order to not become too rigid on the typing of objects. With this, your typing is more oriented towards how objects behave than towards what they are.

Creating a function to apply another one

We are going to create a function that will iterate over a list to apply a function taken as a parameter to all Strings in it.

Time for action – Applying a function on every item

We are going to create a function that will take a function and apply it to every item in a list. We are going to use it to simply display every Int in a list.

1. At first, let's create a function that takes an Int and displays it:

```
class Main
{

    public static function main()
    {
    }

    public static function displayInt(i : Int)
    {
        trace(i);
    }
}
```

2. Then in our `Main` class add a list of `Int`:

```
class Main
{
    public static var intList : List<Int>;

    public static function main()
    {
    intList = new List<Int>(); //Initialize the variable
    }
}
```

3. Note that we have to initialize the list in the main function.

4. Now, let's create the function that will iterate over the list, as follows:

```
public static function iterateAndApply(fun : Int->Void) : Void
{
    for(i in intList)
    {
        fun(i);
    }
}
```

5. Now, we can simply call this function, as follows:

```
iterateAndApply(displayInt)
```

What just happened?

We created an `iterateAndApply` function that takes a method of type `Int->Void`, that is, a method that takes an `Int` and returns nothing.

- The `displayInt` function: We have simply created a function of type `Int->Void` to display an `Int`.

- The `iterateAndApply` function: The most important thing in this function here is that it takes a function of type `Int->Void` as an argument and applies it to every element of the List `intList`.

- The list: We have added a list of `Int` to the `Main` class. What you should note here is that we had to initialize it in the `main` function. Also, after the initialization, you should add some elements to test your application.

Type inference

Type inference is the opposite of explicitly declaring the type of a variable. When using type inference, you simply omit the part telling the type of your variable and let the compiler guess it.

There are several ways for the compiler to guess the type of your variables. Let's see some of them!

Assigning a value

When you assign a value to a variable that still has an unknown type, its type will be inferred as being the one of the assigned value, so for example, if you write:

```
var s;
s = "Hello World";
```

The type of `s` will be inferred to `String`.

Assigning the value of the variable to another one

In addition, if you assign the value of a variable that still has an unknown type to a variable that is of a known type, the type will also be inferred:

```
var s;
var t : String;
t = s;
```

Here, the type of `s` is inferred to `String`.

Passing the variable as a parameter

When you pass a variable to a function, its type is inferred as being the one expected by the function. For example, consider the following code:

```
class Main
{
    static function print(s : String)
    {
        trace(s);
    }
    public static function main()
    {
        var t;
        print(t);
        type(t);
    }
}
```

In this example, t is inferred as being of type String. Note that the type function will print a warning indicating the type of the t variable while compiling.

Casting

There are three ways to cast a type (that is, changing from a type to another one). One is "safe" while the two others are "unsafe".

Safe casting

Doing a safe casting is as simple as using the cast keyword with the syntax cast(variable, Type). Therefore, you can do:

```
var a : A;
var b : B;
b = cast(a, B);
```

This will work if a is in fact an instance of B. If it's not, you will get an error at runtime.

Unsafe casting

You can do an unsafe casting by using the cast keyword in another way. If you just write cast followed by a variable or a value, you can use it as any type. So, for example, the following will compile:

```
var i : Int;
i = cast "Hello";
```

Keep in mind that although this code will compile, it is absolutely possible that depending on the target, it will fail at runtime.

Untyped

It's also possible to completely deactivate type checking in a block of code. To do that, you will use the untyped keyword:

untyped { myVar.doSomething(); }

However, keep in mind that although it will compile, it may also fail at runtime if you do something which is incorrect.

Type parameters

We have already discussed the typing system in haXe, but now, we are going to see the `Type` parameters. You may have already seen them in some languages, maybe under the name of *Generics*.

We will now see:

◆ The usage of `Type` parameters

◆ Using `Type` parameters with already created types

◆ Creating a type that makes use of them

◆ Creating an example

Let's continue discovering the typing system!

Usage of Type parameters

So far, you have only created functions that took some parameters with a defined type and returned a value with a defined type. You have always decided what these types were when creating your functions.

With `Type` parameters, it is possible to let the person use a class and decide what types will be used by some of its functions.

You may wonder why this is useful, and indeed, we have already used `Type` parameters in this book; remember how we said we were going to create an "Array of String"? Well, we have been using `Type` parameters at this moment.

In fact, `Type` parameters are like `function` parameters, but they are given at the class level and instead of waiting for a value, they are waiting for a type.

`Type` parameters can be used for several things, but most of the time, they are used inside containers such as array or list. This way, you can have an array of fully typed elements because you can only add elements of this type and therefore, we can be sure that you only get elements of this type from the array.

Creating a parameterized class

A class is said to be parameterized when it makes uses of `Type` parameters. Therefore, for example, the `Array` class is a parameterized class.

Now, let's see how a part of it may have been written. In this example, I will only talk about the `push` and `shift` methods. The first one allows you to add an object into the array while the last one allows you to remove and retrieve the first object in the array.

Please note that this is not the exact code for the `Array` class.

```
class Array<T>
{
    function new()
    {
        //Do things here
    }

    function push(obj : T)
    {
        //Do things
    }

    function shift() : T
    {
        //Do things
    }
}
```

There are two very important points to notice.

The first one is on the first line, where between the < and > symbol lies an indication telling that our class is parameterized and wants one type to be designed by the T letter. In this class, T is said to be an *abstract* type. Note that you could have used any name, but by convention, we generally use letters starting from T for abstract types.

The other point is that, although the constructor will be called by specifying the parameter type (new Array<String> for example), you do not have to write it in the constructor.

Also, note how in your code you may use T, as if it was an actual type.

The only drawback here is that, as T can be any type, you cannot call any method nor do anything that needs to know the type of the value. This is where constraints will be interesting, and that is what we will discuss now.

Constraint parameters

You can put some constraints on your type parameters. Indeed, you can specify any number of types that the `type` parameters must either implement or extend. Look at the following example:

```
class Fridge<T: (Fruit, Eatable)>
{
    //...
}
```

In this example, the `Fridge` class expects a type that implements or extends both the `Fruit` and `Eatable` types. Note that when you want to impose several constraints on the same abstract type, you have to enclose all of these in parentheses.

Doing so has the following two advantages:

1. As the compiler knows what types your value has, you will be able to use it as if it was typed as being a `Fruit` and an `Eatable`.

2. You can limit the types of values you will accept: for example here, our fridge will only accept fruits that can be eaten.

Extending the fridge

Do you remember that in the earlier chapters, we wrote an example with a fridge? Now, we are going to recreate a `Fridge` class that can only store eatables.

Time for action – A fridge with constraints

Therefore, now our fridge will only be able to access eatable items.

1. First, create a parameterized `Fridge` class that will only accept types implementing the `Eatable` interface:

```
class Fridge<T: Eatable)>
{
    public function new()
    {}
}
```

2. In this class, we will create two methods: an `add` and a `remove` method and we will use an `Array` to store the list of what is inside our `Fridge`:

```
class Fridge<T: Eatable)>
{
    private var items : Array<T>;

    public function new()
    {
        items = new Array<T>(); //Initialize the Array
    }

    public function add(item : T)
    {
        array.push(item);
```

```
    }

    public function remove(item : T)
    {
        array.remove(item);
    }
}
```

For sure, in this state, our fridge is basically just a wrapper around the array class, but now we will do something interesting with it.

3. We will define the `Eatable` interface, so that we can store the date before which the eatable should be eaten, as follows:

```
interface Eatable
{
    public var eatBefore : Date;
}
```

4. Now, add a method to our fridge to dump all eatables that shouldn't be eaten anymore, as follows:

```
public function removeOldItems()
{
    for(eatable in items)
    {
        if(eatable.eatBefore.getTime() <Date.now().getTime())
        //Should've been eaten earlier
        {
            this.remove(eatable);
        }
    }
}
```

What just happened?

In the preceding *Time for action*, we have put to practice what we have seen in this chapter about type parameters and constraints.

◆ **Creating a parameterized class**: We have created the parameterized `Fridge` class, therefore allowing us to add and remove items to and from it, still knowing that they are of a specific type (`T` can represent any type extending or implementing `Eatable`, or even just `Eatable`).

◆ **Adding constraint**: By putting the constraint on the abstract type T, we knew that all objects of this abstract type would be of type Eatable. This allowed us to use the public field defined in the Eatable interface.

Have a go hero – Creating a typed container

Try to create a container for three values (we will create a class with first, second, and third fields to store these values).

These values should be typed, but the class should be able to store any type of values (these should all be of the same type).

Pop quiz – Verify your knowledge

1. A value can have:

   a. One type

   b. Two types

   c. Three types

   d. As many types as we want

2. The safe way to do some casting is:

   a. cast (variable, NewType)

   b. cast variable

   c. untyped { var var2: NewType = variable; }

3. A variable can be typed (2 good answers):

   a. Explicitly

   b. Through inference

   c. Untyped

4. An abstract type can have:

   a. No constraints at all

   b. One constraint at most

   c. Two constraints at most

   d. An unlimited number of constraints

5. A parameterized class with the abstract type T can access methods of objects of type T even if no constraints were put on T:

   a. True

   b. False

Summary

In this chapter, we have learned what the typing system is, how to type variables, how to use type parameters, and how you can put constraints on them. We used different ways to type variable, and learned/showed that using type parameters is up to your preference and your imagination.

Specifically, we covered static typing, inheritance, and type inference. We have also covered function's type and what type parameters are and how to use them to create parameterized classes.

We have covered a great part of the haXe typing system and in the next chapter, we will learn about the Dynamic type, which is one of the most interesting things in haXe!

5

The Dynamic Type and Properties

A magic type.

The Dynamic type is a type with a special behavior. Through this chapter you will learn why, how you can use it, and also what you should pay attention to. Understanding the Dynamic type is a key point in mastering haXe.

We have already been introduced to haXe's typing system. But in this chapter we will learn about something new in this typing system: the Dynamic type. The Dynamic type is a type that introduces a very special behavior that we will now study.

In this chapter we will:

◆ Use Dynamic variables

◆ Learn about Dynamic's pitfalls

◆ Learn about the parameterized Dynamic class

◆ Implement Dynamic in a class

◆ Learn about the use of properties in classes

◆ Implement properties in classes

Let's get started.

Freeing yourself from the typing system

The goal of the Dynamic type is to allow one to free oneself from the typing system. In fact, when you define a variable as being a Dynamic type, this means that the compiler won't make any kind of type checking on this variable.

Time for action – Assigning to Dynamic variables

When you declare a variable as being Dynamic, you will be able to assign any value to it at **compile time**. So you can actually compile this code:

```
class DynamicTest
{
    public static function main()
    {
        var dynamicVar : Dynamic;
        dynamicVar = "Hello";
        dynamicVar = 123;
        dynamicVar = {name:"John", lastName : "Doe"};
        dynamicVar = new Array<String>();
    }
}
```

The compiler won't mind even though you are assigning values with different types to the same variable!

Time for action – Assigning from Dynamic variables

You can assign the content of any Dynamic variable to a variable of any type. Indeed, we generally say that the Dynamic type can be used in place of any type and that a variable of type Dynamic is indeed of any type.

So, with that in mind, you can now see that you can write and compile this code:

```
class DynamicTest
{
    public static function main()
    {
        var dynamicVar : Dynamic;
        var year : Int;
        dynamicVar = "Hello";
        year = dynamicVar;
    }
}
```

So, here, even though we will indeed assign a String to a variable typed as `Int`, the compiler won't complain. But you should keep in mind that this is only at compile time! If you abuse this possibility, you may get some strange behavior!

Field access

A Dynamic variable has an infinite number of fields all of Dynamic type. That means you can write the following:

```
class DynamicTest
{
   public static function main()
   {
      var dynamicVar : Dynamic;
      dynamicVar = {};
      dynamicVar.age = 12; //age is Dynamic
      dynamicVar.name = "Benjamin"; //name is Dynamic
   }
}
```

Note that whether this code will work or not at runtime is highly dependent on the runtime you're targeting.

Functions in Dynamic variables

It is also possible to store functions in Dynamic variables and to call them:

```
class DynamicTest
{
   public static function main()
   {
      var dynamicVar : Dynamic;
      dynamicVar = function (name : String) { trace("Hello" + name); };
      dynamicVar();

      var dynamicVar2 : Dynamic = {};
      dynamicVar2.sayBye = function (name : String) { trace("Bye" +
        name ); };
      dynamicVar2.sayBye();
   }
}
```

As you can see, it is possible to assign functions to a Dynamic variable or even to one of its fields. It's then possible to call them as you would do with any function.

Again, even though this code will compile, its success at running will depend on your target.

Parameterized Dynamic class

You can parameterize the Dynamic class to slightly modify its behavior. When parameterized, every field of a Dynamic variable will be of the given type.

Let's see an example:

```
class DynamicTest
{
    public static function main()
    {
        var dynamicVar : Dynamic<String>;
        dynamicVar = {};
        dynamicVar.name = "Benjamin"; //name is a String
        dynamicVar.age = 12; //Won't compile since age is a String
    }
}
```

In this example, `dynamicVar.name` and `dynamicVar.age` are of type `String`, therefore, this example will fail to compile on line 7 because we are trying to assign an `Int` to a `String`.

Classes implementing Dynamic

A class can implement a Dynamic, parameterized or not.

Time for action – Implementing a non-parameterized Dynamic

When one implements a non-parameterized Dynamic in a class, one will be able to access an infinite number of fields in an instance. All fields that are not declared in the class will be of type Dynamic.

So, for example:

```
class User implements Dynamic
{
    public var name : String;
    public var age : Int;
    //...
}
//...
var u = new User(); //u is of type User
u.name = "Benjamin"; //String
u.age = 22; //Int
u.functionrole = "Author"; //Dynamic
```

What just happened?

As you can see, the `functionrole` field is not declared in the `User` class, so it is of type Dynamic.

In fact, when you try to access a field that's not declared in the class, a function named `resolve` will be called and it will get the name of the property accessed. You can then return the value you want. This can be very useful to implement some magic things.

Time for action – Implementing a parameterized Dynamic

When implementing a parameterized Dynamic, you will get the same behavior as with a non-parameterized Dynamic except that the fields that are not declared in the class will be of the type given as a parameter.

Let's take almost the same example but with a parameterized Dynamic:

```
class User implements Dynamic<String>
{
    public var name : String;
    public var age : Int;
    //...
}
//...
var u = new User(); //u is of type User
u.name = "Benjamin"; //String
u.age = 22; //Int
u.functionrole = "Author"; //String because of the type parameter
```

What just happened?

As you can see here, fields that are not declared in the class are of type `String` because we gave `String` as a type parameter.

Using a resolve function when implementing Dynamic

Now we are going to use what we've just learned. We are going to implement a `Component` class that will be instantiated from a configuration file.

A component will have properties and metadata. Such properties and metadata are not pre-determined, which means that the properties' names and values will be read from the configuration file.

Each line of the configuration file will hold the name of the property or metadata, its value, and a 0 if it's a property (or otherwise it will be a metadata). Each of these fields will be separated by a space.

The last constraint is that we should be able to read the value of a property or metadata by using the dot-notation.

Time for action – Writing our Component class

As you may have guessed, we will begin with a very simple Component class — all it has to do at first is to have two Hashes: one for metadata, the other one for properties.

```
class Component
{
    public var properties : Hash<String>;
    public var metadata : Hash<String>;

    public function new()
    {
        properties = new Hash<String>();
        metadata = new Hash<String>();
    }
}
```

It is that simple at the moment.

As you can see, we do not implement access via the dot-notation at the moment. We will do it later, but the class won't be very complicated even with the support for this notation.

Time for action – Parsing the configuration file

We are now going to parse our configuration file to create a new instance of the Component class.

In order to do that, we are going to create a ComponentParser class. It will contain two functions:

◆ parseConfigurationFile to parse a configuration file and return an instance of Component.

◆ writeConfigurationFile that will take an instance of Component and write data to a file.

Let's see how our class should look at the moment (this example will only work on neko):

```
class ComponentParser
{
    /**
    *   This function takes a path to a configuration file and returns
          an instance of ComponentParser
    */
    public static function parseConfigurationFile(path : String)
    {
        var stream = neko.io.File.read(path, false); //Open our file for
          reading in character mode
        var comp = new Component(); //Create a new instance of Component
        while(!stream.eof()) //While we're not at the end of the file
        {
            var str = stream.readLine(); //Read one line from file
            var fields = str.split(" "); //Split the string using space
              as delimiter
            if(fields[2] == "0")
            {
                comp.properties.set(fields[0], fields[1]); //Set the
                  key<->value in the properties Hash
            } else
            {
                comp.metadata.set(fields[0], fields[1]); //Set the
                  key<->value in the metadata Hash
            }
        }
        stream.close();
        return comp;
    }
}
```

It's not that complicated, and you would actually use the same kind of method if you were going to use a XML file.

Time for action – Testing our parser

Before continuing any further, we should test our parser in order to be sure that it works as expected.

To do this, we can use the following configuration file:

```
nameMyComponent 1
textHelloWorld 0
```

If everything works as expected, we should have a name metadata with the value `MyComponent` and a property named text with the value HelloWorld.

Let's write a simple test class:

```
class ComponentImpl
{
    public static function main(): Void
    {
        var comp = ComponentParser.parseConfigurationFile("conf.txt");
        trace(comp.properties.get("text"));
        trace(comp.metadata.get("name"));
    }
}
```

Now, if everything went well, while running this program, you should get the following output:

```
ComponentImpl.hx:6: HelloWorld
ComponentImpl.hx:7: MyComponent
```

Time for action – Writing the configuration file

Now, let's write a function in ComponentParser to write a configuration file from an instance of Component. So here is our class completed:

```
class ComponentParser
{
    /**
    *   This function takes a path to a configuration file and returns
    *       an instance of ComponentParser
    */
    public static function parseConfigurationFile(path : String)
    {
        var stream = neko.io.File.read(path, false); //Open our file for
            reading in character mode
        var comp = new Component(); //Create a new instance of Component
        while(!stream.eof()) //While we're not at the end of the file
        {
            var str = stream.readLine(); //Read one line from file
            var fields = str.split(" "); //Split the string using space
                as delimiter
            if(fields[2] == "0")
            {
                comp.properties.set(fields[0], fields[1]); //Set the
                    key<->value in the properties Hash
            } else
            {
                comp.metadata.set(fields[0], fields[1]); //Set the
                    key<->value in the metadata Hash
```

```
        }
      }
      stream.close();
      return comp;
  }
  /**
   *  This function takes a path to a configuration file.
   *  It also takes an instance of Component to save.
   */
  public static function writeConfigurationFile
     (path : String, comp : Component)
  {
     var stream = neko.io.File.write(path, false); //Open our file
        for writing in character mode
     //Let's iterate over metadata
     for(meta in comp.metadata.keys())
     {
        //Write the meta's name, a space, its value, and a space
           followed by 1 and new-line
        stream.writeString(meta + " " + comp.metadata.get
           (meta) + " 1\n");
     }
     //Let's iterate over properties
     for(prop in comp.properties.keys())
     {
        //Write the properties name, a space, its value, and a space
           followed by 0 and new-line
        stream.writeString(prop + " " + comp.properties.get
           (prop) + " 0\n");
     }
     stream.close();
  }
}
```

As you can see, the new function is pretty simple too.

Time for action – Testing the writer

A good way to test our newly created function is to continue after our first test and just save the result of `parseConfigurationFile`.

So, here is the new test class:

```
class ComponentImpl
{
```

```
public static function main(): Void
{
    var comp = ComponentParser.parseConfigurationFile
        ("bin/conf.txt");
    trace(comp.properties.get("text"));
    trace(comp.metadata.get("name"));

    //Test writing
    ComponentParser.writeConfigurationFile("bin/out.txt", comp);
}
}
```

After running this test, you should get a file with the following content:

```
nameMyComponent 1
textHelloWorld 0
```

As you saw, that was really simple.

The dot-notation

If you remember, one constraint was to be able to read values of metadata and properties using the dot-notation.

In fact, everything we've done until now has been done only for the sake of this exercise and for you to write some haXe code.

Although this is important, let's move on to implementing access via the dot-notation.

To do that, we will make our class implement Dynamic<String> and implement a resolve method.

Before doing that, there's just one question that arises: how are we going to handle the situation if a key exists in the metadata Hash and in the properties Hash? In our example, we will handle this situation quite easily by simply returning the value that is in the metadata.

So, here is our Component class modified:

```
class Component implements Dynamic<String>
{
    public var properties : Hash<String>;
    public var metadata : Hash<String>;

    public function new()
    {
        properties = new Hash<String>();
        metadata = new Hash<String>();
```

```
    }
    public function resolve(name : String) : String
    {
        //If this key exists in the metadata
        if(metadata.exists(name))
            returnmetadata.get(name);
        //If this key exists as a property
        if(properties.exists(name))
            returnproperties.get(name);
        //This key doesn't exist, return null.
        return null;
    }
}
```

Note how we added a "implements Dynamic<String>" and the signature of the resolve function.

When we write `comp.someName` it is as if we had written comp. resolve (`"someName"`) as the compiler makes the transformation automatically.

Thoughts on writing our parser

As you can see, although the proposed subject of this exercise was pretty long, it was pretty easy to implement what we were asked to implement.

Also, the longest part of it indeed was to implement the ComponentParser class and not to implement the dot-notation in order to access metadata and properties.

The dynamic keyword

In haXe code you will sometimes meet the dynamic keyword (all in lowercase). It doesn't have a lot of things to do with the Dynamic type and only appears when declaring a function. It does mean that a method can be rebound. That is, it is possible to change the body of the function.

This keyword is necessary because on some platforms, those methods have to be generated in a special way that can induce some cost on performance.

Here is an example of how to declare such a function:

```
public dynamic function myFunction()
{
    //Do things
}
```

Warning

In this chapter we've talked about the Dynamic type. We've been discussing this all through the chapter, but it is important to say it again: the Dynamic type is there to tell the compiler not to do any type checking.

Although the compiler won't complain, it doesn't mean that your code will run correctly. It will depend on the runtime. So, if you're targeting JavaScript which is a dynamic language it is likely that it will work without any problem, but if you're targeting a more static runtime there are chances that you will get into troubles for using Dynamic too much.

Most of the time, Dynamic is used when trying to use some native features of the runtime you're targeting or for interoperability purposes. It can also be used sometimes just to ease development.

It is highly advised to limit the usage of Dynamic as much as possible to avoid problems.

Properties in classes

We have talked a lot about the Dynamic type, but now, we are going to talk about something else: properties.

Use

Sometimes, you would like to be able to react to the access to an object's property. Whether this is when reading from or assigning to the property, the only way to do that is through the use of functions.

It would then be possible to use it with some code looking like this:

```
myObject.getValue();
//or
myObject.setValue("This is my new value");
```

This is a non-natural way of accessing properties, and it can make the code really difficult to read, particularly if you are going to chain calls.

With properties, we will be able to define our functions `setValue` and `getValue` so that we can react to accesses to our properties. But what is so interesting with properties, is that we won't have to directly call our functions, we will just be able to access properties as if they were simple fields:

```
myObject.value;
//or
myObject.value = "This is my new value";
```

This syntax is really more natural and easier to read.

Implementation

Implementing properties is not something very complicated. As you may guess, you will have to write your two accessors (the functions to get and set the value). After writing them, you will have to bind them to the property. All of this will be done easily in haXe.

Writing the getter

The getter of a property is the function that will get called when the user wants to read from your property. This function should take no arguments and return a value of the same type as your property.

Here is a simple example:

```
public function getWidth() : Int
{
    return width;
}
```

For sure, simply doing that does not have any interest over accessing a simple field, but it's up to you to use properties whenever needed.

Writing the setter

If you need to write a setter for your property, you will need to keep two important things in mind:

◆ Your setter will take one argument that will be of the type of your property

◆ Your setter will return a value of the type of your property

Because the first point is easy to remember, as this argument will be used to give you the value the user wants to assign to your property, you may really wonder why the second point is needed. Well, the reason is simple; here is some simple code to demonstrate it:

```
a.value = b.value = c.value
```

In this example, the `b.value` gets assigned the value of the `c.value` and then the `a.value` gets assigned the new value of the `b.value`. This code would get transformed to the following if value is a property with the `setValue` as the setter:

```
a.setValue( b.setValue( c.getValue ) );
```

When seeing this, it becomes obvious that the setter needs to return the new value of the property.

Here is a sample code to demonstrate how this could be implemented:

```
public function setWidth(value : Int) : Int
{
    if(value >= 0)
    {
        width = value;
        //Maybe you will want to do some other things to react to the
           assignment
    }
    return width;}
```

This code actually implements a setter for our width property that will verify that the new value is superior or equal to 0. This actually makes sense for a width since a negative width doesn't make any sense.

Defining the property

So we've seen how to implement the getter and the setter for a property but we now need to define this property.

The syntax to do this is pretty close to the one used to declare a field. The only difference is that we will provide a reference to our getter and to our setter:

```
public var width(getWidth, setWidth) : Int;
```

This one was easy, but we will now see how we can do some more advanced things such as forbidding getting or setting a property's value.

Accessibility

Until now, we have created a property that had a getter and a setter that we wrote.

But it is possible to write a property that has no getter or no setter. In order to do this, we will simply write "null" in place of the getter or setter reference.

So, here is an example of a property that would be accessible only to read:

```
public var readOnly(getProp, null) : String;
```

Here is an example of a property that would only be writeable:

```
public var writeOnly(null, setProp) : String;
```

The default getter

If your getter is simply going to return the value of your field, you may want to use the default setter. This way, you won't have to write such a simple function.

So, for example:

```
var prop(default, setX) : Int;
```

This will tell the compiler to directly access the prop field when reading the property's value.

The default setter

As you can use a default getter, you can also use a default setter. The default setter will simply assign the new value to the field and return it.

So, for example:

```
var prop(getX, default) : Int;
```

This will tell the compiler to directly access the prop field when writing the property's value.

The dynamic getter and setter

When defining your property, you can also set your getter or setter to dynamic.

If you do so, you will be able to redefine the functions used as setter and getter by using Reflect.setField. To do so, you will have to set the fields "set_" and "get_" followed by the name of your property.

The never getter and setter

When using null as a setter or getter, the class the property is defined in can indeed read or write the value of this property. The operation is only forbidden out of the class.

It is possible to completely forbid an access to a getter or setter by using the never getter or setter.

A compile-time feature

Properties are a compile-time feature; what this means is that when you access a property, the compiler knows that it indeed is a property and knows what setter and getter it refers to. This way, when compiling, the compiler will automatically create a call to the functions.

The only drawback to this approach is that if the compiler doesn't know the type of your variable it won't be able to generate those calls.

So, to sum-up things, in an untyped block and with a variable typed as Dynamic, the compiler won't have a clue that you are accessing a property and not a simple field and, therefore, won't be able to generate function calls.

Have a go hero – Writing a person class

Imagine that you have to write a class that represents a person. A person can be given a name when he/she comes to life but it is impossible to change it afterwards. Try to write a class to represent that (but it should still be possible to read the name).

Pop Quiz – Doing the things

1. A Dynamic has:
   a. A pre-defined set of fields.
   b. An unlimited number of fields.
   c. A limited number of fields that can change.

2. To be able to change the body of a function:
   a. You have to use the dynamic keyword.
   b. You don't have to do anything.

Summary

In this chapter we learned about the Dynamic type and the dynamic keyword.

Specifically, we covered what the Dynamic type is, what the parameterized Dynamic type is, and how you can implement both in your own classes. We also covered how you can use properties.

Dynamics can be useful but remember to avoid overuse them as they can break your code at runtime.

On the same note, remember that properties are a compile-time feature only.

In the next chapter, we are going to learn about other things in the typing system such as Enums and Interfaces.

6
Using and Writing Interfaces, Typedefs, and Enums

Interfaces, Typedefs, and Enums.

In this chapter, we will discover three new points in the haXe typing system. We will see how they are different from what you may be used to in other languages such as C# or JAVA.

In this chapter we will talk about interfaces. We've already encountered them but we will clarify some points and learn more about them. We will also learn about typedefs and extensions. Finally, we'll be talking about enums that are quite advanced in haXe.

In this chapter, we will:

- ◆ Learn how to write an interface
- ◆ Learn about some important interfaces such as iterables, iterators, and haxe.rtti
- ◆ Learn what typedefs are and how to express them
- ◆ Learn what enums are
- ◆ Learn how to switch them over

We will practice all of the above using several examples.

Interfaces

Interfaces contain no instructions to be executed and only describe what functions and properties a class implementing it should expose.

Purpose

You may wonder what interfaces may be useful for since they contain no instructions to be executed.

Well indeed, sometimes you just want to get an object that's able to do some things for example, let's say you are writing an application that has to handle the sequencing of some animations. You do not really care how an animation is implemented (that is, what instructions it contains), what you want to do is be able to start it, stop it, and go to a position in it, but you do not care how the animation handles all these actions.

This is a typical case where interfaces will be used. In our example, we could create a "Playable" interface (that's a pretty good name although it does define other possibilities). This interface will define several functions:

Function's name	Function's type
start	Void->Void
stop	Void->Void
goto	Int->Void

It will also define what should be a public variable to get a name for the animation and a variable to store a callback (a reference to a function to call) when the animation ends with:

Variable	Type
name	String
endCallback	Void->Void

Here is how we will write this interface:

```
interface Playable
{
    function start() : Void;
    function stop() : Void;
    function goto(position : Int) : Void;

    var name : String;
    var endCallback : Void->Void;
}
```

As you can see, it's not that complicated. Indeed, it does look a lot like writing a class except that you don't write the implementation of functions.

Default visibility

Well, indeed, it does look like writing a class but there are some differences. First, let's discuss about the visibility of members. In classes members are private by default, while in interfaces they are public by default.

In fact, that does make sense as you will primarily use interfaces to describe what interface objects should offer to interact with others.

Still, it's possible to tell that some members can be declared private by simply writing "private" before them as you would do in a class.

Type inference

As you do not write any instructions in interfaces it would be impossible for the compiler to infer the type of members. This is why, as you can see in the preceding code, you have to explicitly declare the type of the members.

Implementing an interface

For an interface to be useful it has to be implemented by some class. Implementing an interface means exposing it to other classes and having statements for the functions described in it. For example, here is a very minimalistic class implementing our `Playable` interface:

```
class UselessAnimation implements Playable
{
   public var name : String;
   public var endCallback : Void->Void;

   public function start() : Void
   {
      trace("I'm starting.");
      endCallback();
   }

   public function stop() : Void
   {
      trace("I'm stopping.");
   }

   public function goto(pos : Int)
   {
      trace("I'm going to position " + Std.string(pos));
   }

   public function new()
   {}
}
```

Implementation and type inference

Although, implementation and type inference are not depicted in the preceding code it is possible to omit writing types and count on type inference when implementing an interface. The only constraint you have is that the types should be inferred to those defined by the interface or else the compiler will complain.

Implementation and visibility

When implementing an interface it is easy to forget to add the public keyword in front of your members either because you are reading the interface declaration or because you are just copying and pasting it.

Although, it's not an important error and the compiler will tell you about it, it's good to keep in mind that even though you are implementing an interface, in classes the members are private unless specified otherwise.

Making use of interfaces

When you are defining an interface, you create a new type, exactly like when you are creating an interface. Also, classes implementing that interface will be of the type defined by this interface. This means that interfaces can be used like any other type.

Let's do a quick implementation of our `Sequencer`:

```
class Sequencer
{
    public var animations : Array<Playable>;
    public var currentlyPlaying : Playable;

    public function new()
    {
        animations = new Array<Playable>(); //Initialize array
    }

    public function start()
    {
        if(currentlyPlaying != null)
            return; //Something's already playing, do nothing

        if(animations.length==0)
            return; //There's nothing left to be played, do nothing

        currentlyPlaying = animations.shift(); //Get the first animation
            and remove it from array
```

```
            currentlyPlaying.endCallback = this.nextSequence;
            trace("Starting playing animation " + currentlyPlaying.name);
            currentlyPlaying.start();
        }

        public function nextSequence()
        {
            if(currentlyPlaying != null)
                currentlyPlaying.stop(); //If something is playing stop it

            currentlyPlaying = null;
            start();
        }

        public function addItem(animation : Playable)
        {
            this.animations.push(animation);
        }
    }
```

It is a pretty simple implementation that has an Array of `Playable` to keep a reference to what's left to play, a `nextSequence` function to continue to the next animation and an `addItem` function to add an animation to play.

Now let's quickly write a main function to test it:

```
    class Main
    {
        public static function main(): Void
        {
            var anim1 = new UselessAnimation();
            anim1.name = "Animation 1";
            var anim2 = new UselessAnimation();
            anim2.name = "Animation 2";

            var sequencer = new Sequencer();
            sequencer.addItem(anim1);
            sequencer.addItem(anim2);

            sequencer.start();
        }
    }
```

As you can see we do not type objects as `UselessAnimation` in the `Sequencer` class, but as `Playable` and we are able to use all methods and variables defined in the `Playable` interface. This is because `UselessAnimation` implements `Playable`. We know it will have all its members.

Typedefs

Typedefs are created using the typedef keyword. They allow you to define a type without having to create a class or an interface. They indeed can be used for several things.

Time for action – Naming Anonymous Types

We've already talked about Anonymous Types; with typedefs it is possible to give them a name. This avoids the need to rewrite the complete type definition each time you want to make reference to an anonymous type.

Imagine that we have the following code:

```
class Greetings
{
    public function new()
    {}

    public function sayHiTo(obj : {name : String})
    {
        trace("Hi " + obj.name);
    }

    public static function main()
    {
        var paul = {name : "Paul"};
        var d = new Greetings();
        d.sayHiTo(paul);
    }
}
```

And that we want to rewrite it so that we don't have to rewrite the definition of `{name : String}` everywhere but instead use the `HasName` name to refer to it.

We are simply going to write the definition for our type and use it where needed:

```
class Greetings
{
    public function new()
```

```
    {}

    public function sayHiTo(obj : HasName)
    {
        trace("Hi " + obj.name);
    }

    public static function main()
    {
        var paul = {name : "Paul"};
        var d = new Greetings();
        d.sayHiTo(paul);
    }
}

typedef HasName =
{
    name : String
};
```

What just happened?

We have written the `HasName` typedef and used it when defining the `sayHiTo` function.

Note that the syntax is a bit different from the one used for classes or interfaces; you should notice that one has to write the equal sign after the typedef's name.

As you can see, it has been possible to replace the Anonymous Type in the signature of the `sayHiTo` function by the name of the typedef. But in fact, it will behave in the same way.

The only drawback is that it doesn't offer a shortcut for creating an anonymous object of the given type. This is why we still have to repeat the structure of the type when creating our Paul variable.

Aliases

We've just seen that by using typedefs it is possible to somewhat give a name to an anonymous type.

In fact, typedefs can be used as aliases for any type. This way it is possible to, for example, give a short name to a type that has a very long name. For example:

```
class VeryLongClassName
{
    var id : String;
```

```
    var age : Int;

    public static function main()
    {
       var my_vlcn = new VeryLongClassName();
       my_vlcn.age = 23;
       my_vlcn.id = "someid";
       printInfos(my_vlcn);
    }

    public static function printInfos(vlcn : VeryLongClassName)
    {
       trace(vlcn.id + " is " + vlcn.age + " years old.");
    }

    public static function new()
    {}
}
```

We could make use of typedefs to shorten `VeryLongClassName` into `VLCN`:

```
class VeryLongClassName
{
    var id : String;
    var age : Int;

    public static function main()
    {
       var my_vlcn = new VLCN();
       my_vlcn.age = 23;
       my_vlcn.id = "someid";
       printInfos(my_vlcn);
    }

    public static function printInfos(vlcn : VLCN)
    {
       trace(vlcn.id + " is " + vlcn.age + " years old.");
    }

    public static function new()
    {}
}

typedef VLCN = VeryLongClassName;
```

Note that not only can VLCN be used where the VeryLongClassName type was expected, but it is also possible to use it where the VeryLongClassName class (for example, when constructing our my_vlcn object) was expected.

Although typedefs as aliases may be useful, you should make sure that your naming will make sense and you shouldn't abuse them as that could really obfuscate your code.

Visibility

Typedefs are public by default. That means they can be used from anywhere. So, for example, if in MyTypes.hx you have a typedef defined as:

```
typedef User =
{
   name : String,
   age : Int
}
```

You can access it by using an import:

```
import MyTypes;

class SomeClass
{
   public static function main()
   {
      var u : User;
   }
}
```

Or by using its full access path:

```
class SomeClass
{
   public static function main()
   {
      var u : MyTypes.User;
   }
}
```

This is for publicly visible typedefs.

Private typedefs

A typedef can be marked as private:

```
private typedef User =
{
    name : String,
    age : Int
}
```

In this case, it will be available only in the module in which it is declared. There will be no way to access it from outside this module, but on the other hand, it will be possible to declare typedefs with the same name in the same package. In this case it is better if they are all private in order to prevent hiding one that will be public.

This can prove to be useful if you want, for example, to create some aliases to a type that you're going to use a lot in your module but do not want it to interfere with the rest of your application's code.

Duck typing

We've already talked about duck typing and Anonymous Types. As you remember, duck typing refers to the idea that if something walks and makes noise like a duck, then it must be a duck. In code, this is materialized by the fact that if some object has a defined set of members then it must be of the required type.

Let's take our example from *Naming Anonymous Types* and modify it a bit—we will add a User class, and in our main function instead of creating an anonymous object, we will create an instance of this User class. This will be our new code:

```
class Greetings
{
    public function new()
    {}

    public function sayHiTo(obj : HasName)
    {
        trace("Hi " + obj.name);
    }

    public static function main()
    {
        var paul = new User();
        var d = new Greetings();
        d.sayHiTo(paul);
    }
```

```
    }

    typedef HasName =
    {
        name : String
    }

    class User
    {
        public var name : String;
        public var age  : Int;

        public function new()
        {
            name = "";
            age = 0;
        }
    }
```

As you can see we can pass our instance of User to the sayHiTo function that expects an object of type HasName. This is possible although the User class doesn't explicitly implement HasName because HasName makes reference to an Anonymous Type and therefore supports duck typing.

Note that that wouldn't work if HasName was not referencing an Anonymous Type.

Typedefs to access private members

Although, typedefs to access private members may seem a bit strange, they can be used to access private members of an object without going the untyped way.

In fact, typedefs can contain private members, but unlike when a member of a class or an interface is private, those can still be accessed publicly. They are declared private only so that the signature of your type matches one of the types that contains a private member that you want to access.

Well, an example is worth a thousand words so, here it is:

```
    class User
    {
        public var name : String;
        private var age  : Int;

        public function new()
        {}
```

```
}

typedef PublicUser =
{
   public var name : String;
   private var age : Int;
}

class Start
{
   public static function main()
   {
      var people : PublicUser = new User();
      people.name = "Somebody";
      people.age = 38;

      trace(people.age);
   }
}
```

See how we can access people's age? That's because we've declared it of type `PublicUser` and not of type `User`. The people variable accepts to be assigned a `User` because of duck typing.

Also note the syntax we've had to use in our typedef. It is pretty close to an interface definition.

Creating iterable objects

Iterable objects are objects that you can iterate when using a `for` loop such as:

```
for(item in obj) {}
```

Here, `obj` is an iterable.

An iterable is a typedef that only contains a function iterator of type `Void->Iterator`, which means that this function will return an object of type **Iterator**.

An iterator is a typedef too. It is made up of two functions:

◆ The first one is `hasNext` which is of type `Void-> Bool`, this function returns true if there's any other object to be returned (a new value for our "item" variable in our preceding example) or false otherwise.

- The second function is named `Next`. It takes no parameters and returns the next value. It's as simple as that. So, here is a simple **Iterator** example:

```
class IntIterator
{
   private var end : Int;
   private var current : Int;

   public function new(start : Int, end : Int)
   {
      this.current = start;
      this.end = end;
   }

   public function hasNext() : Bool
   {
      if(current+1 <= end)
      {
         return true;
      } else
      {
         return false;
      }
   }

   public function next()
   {
      return ++current;
   }
}
```

This iterator will return all integer values between start (not included) and end (included).

Enums

Enums exist in various modern languages and you may have already met them. But there are some chances that you didn't meet enums as they are in haXe.

Basic enums

Enums exist in haXe as they exist in most languages and you'll use them when you want to choose a value in a determined list of possibilities. For example, you may have something like this:

```
enum BasicColor
{
    red;
    blue;
    green;
    yellow;
    black;
    white;
}
```

When expecting a `BasicColor` you will have to pick a color in the list of choices.

This is what you certainly are used to doing with enums. But haXe has more to offer.

Enums' constructors

What may surprise you if you are used to enums in some other languages is that in haXe, an enums values are not constants, they are real objects (and we will see later that they can even have some properties). In fact, each choice in your list of values is a constructor.

So, an enum has several constructors and limits you to the construction of values defined by these constructors.

Switching on basic enums

Imagine you want to test which choice has been made in an enum, the most straightforward way to do it is to use `switch`.

Let's see a quick example using `BasicColor`:

```
class Start
{
    public static function main()
    {
        trace(fromBasicColorToString(BasicColor.blue));
    }

    public static function fromBasicColorToString(color : BasicColor)
    {
        switch(color)
```

```
        {
            case red:
                return "red";
            case blue:
                return "blue";
            case green:
                return "green";
            case yellow:
                return "yellow";
            case black:
                return "black";
            case white:
                return "white";
        }
    }
}
```

Although, this is not really visible since we are using return, you do not have to write `break` at the end of a case.

There's also the possibility to define a default case in case none of the other cases defined match:

```
class Start
{
    public static function main()
    {
        trace(fromBasicColorToString(BasicColor.blue));
    }

    public static function fromBasicColorToString(color : BasicColor)
    {
        switch(color)
        {
            case red:
                return "red";
            case blue:
                return "blue";
            case green:
                return "green";
            default:
                return "You didn't use red, nor blue, nor green.";
        }
    }
}
```

```
enum BasicColor
{
    red;
    blue;
    green;
    yellow;
    black;
    white;
}
```

As you can see in this example, if we choose a value other than red, blue, and green, we will fall into the default case.

Also note that you don't have to write `case` before the default word.

Enums with parameters

What you define in an enum are indeed constructors. Well, as any constructor, they can take parameters. This will allow you to give more information on the value you want.

Continuing with our example of colors, you may know that there are several ways to construct a color; two common ways are using RGB notation and RGBA notation. This could be represented with an enum as the following:

```
enum Color
{
    RGB(r : Int, g : Int, b : Int);
    RGBA(r : Int, g : Int, b : Int, a : Int);
}
```

As you can see, it does look like we are defining constructors but with names different from "new".

Of course, you can switch over these enums and get the values that have been passed to the constructor.

Time for action – Switching over enums with parameters

Switching over an enum that has parameters is done in the same way as switching over a basic enum. The only difference is that we will have to write the names of the parameters in order to get them.

Imagine that we have an enum representing a color either as RGB or RGBA and that we want to get the string representing this color.

1. First, let's write our enum:

```
enum Color
{
    rgb(r : Int, g : Int, b : Int);
    rgba(r : Int, g : Int, b : Int, a : Int);
}
```

2. Now, let's write our switch:

```
public static function fromColorToString(color :Color)
{
    switch(color)
    {
        case rgb(r, g, b):
            return "RGB(" + r + "," + g + ", " + b + ")";
        case rgba(r, g, b, a):
            return "RGB(" + r + "," + g + ", " + b + "," + a + ")";
    }
}
```

What just happened?

In the second step, we got parameters from the color so that we could construct the string.

As you can see, you don't need to rewrite the types of the parameters in your switch statement. But there's one more thing you should pay attention to: you have to keep the same names for parameters in your switch statement than the one used when declaring the enum.

It is also possible to mix constructors with and without parameters in the same enum. In this case, when you switch it over, make sure not to put parentheses after the name of the constructors that do not have parameters.

Have a go hero – Write a fridge with an iterator

With what we've seen in this chapter you should be able to do something quite simple:

Let's write a `Fridge` class that can take and store any object that has a `useBy` date, a name, and a property to remember at what `Date` it's been stored in the fridge.

Then, iterate over items in the fridge just by writing something such as "for(item in fridge)".

Time for action – Writing our Fridge class

Now, let's start writing our `Fridge` class.

Let's start of easily by just implementing it so that it has a list of storables in which to store our items:

```
package fridgeManager;

class Fridge
{
    public var storedItems : List<Storable>;

    public function new()
    {
        storedItems = new List<Storable>();
    }

    public function addItem(item : Storable)
    {
        storedItems.push(item);
        item.storedOn = Date.now();
    }

    public function removeItem(item : Storable)
    {
        storedItems.remove(item);
        item.storedOn = null;
    }

}
```

What just happened?

Now, we have two methods to manage items in the fridge: `addItem` and `removeItem`.

The `addItem` function will add the item to the list and update its `storedOn` property. The `removeItem` function will set `storedOn` to null as the object isn't stored anymore.

Time for action – Making it possible to iterate over a fridge

Now, everything is working as expected but we want to add the possibility to iterate over our Fridge.

1. For that to happen, as we have seen before, we need to have an iterator function that will take no argument and return an iterator. So let's write it:

```
public function iterator()
{
    return new StorableIterator(this);
}
```

2. Since this is declared in the iterable typedef, we don't have to mark our class as implementing iterable. So our class now looks like this:

```
package fridgeManager;

class Fridge
{
    public var storedItems : List<Storable>;

    public function new()
    {
        storedItems = new List<Storable>();
    }

    public function addItem(item : Storable)
    {
        storedItems.push(item);
        item.storedOn = Date.now();
    }

    public function removeItem(item : Storable)
    {
        storedItems.remove(item);
        item.storedOn = null;
    }

    public function iterator()
    {
        return new StorableIterator(this);
    }
}
```

What just happened?

We have made our `Fridge` iterable now by adding the iterator function.

The `StorableIterator` is a new class we're going to create right now.

Time for action – Creating the iterator

We now have a function in our `Fridge` to return an iterator, but we still need to write this iterator. To keep things simple in this exercise, we will simply rely on the iterator of the Fridge's list.

Now, we will create this `StorableIterator` class:

```
package fridgeManager;

class StorableIterator
{
    private var iterator : Iterator<Storable>;

    public function hasNext() : Bool
    {
        return iterator.hasNext();
    }

    public function next() : Storable
    {
        return iterator.next();
    }

    public function new(fridge : Fridge)
    {
        iterator = fridge.storedItems.iterator();
    }
}
```

What just happened?

As you can see it is pretty simple and relies on the fridge list's iterator.

Just remember that the `hasNext` function returns a `Bool` stating whether there's any item left to iterate, and the next function returns the next item.

In the constructor, we just store the fridge list's iterator.

Since iterator is a typedef, we do not have to say that our class implements it. The compiler will know it by itself.

Our main function

Now we will create a simple main function in order to test whether everything works as expected.

In this function, we will create our `Fridge`, create two items, and add them in the fridge. Then we will iterate over our fridge:

```
class FridgeManager
{
    private static var fridge : fridgeManager.Fridge;

    public static function main(): Void
    {
        fridge = new fridgeManager.Fridge();

        var myDrink = new fridgeManager.Drink();
        myDrink.name = "Benjamin's drink";

        var myFood = new fridgeManager.Food();
        myFood.name = "Benjamin's food";

        fridge.addItem(myDrink);
        fridge.addItem(myFood);

        //Let's display what's inside the fridge:
        for(stored in fridge)
        {
            trace(stored.name);
        }
    }
}
```

Pop quiz – Typedef, interfaces, and Enums

1. Is it possible for the compiler to be able to do type inference inside interfaces?

    a. Yes, it is possible

    b. Yes, but only if the interface is implemented in a class

    c. No, it is not possible

2. How can enums be defined in haXe?

    a. They they are defined as a set of limited possible values

    b. They are defined as strings

    c. They are defined as Ints/interfaces

    d. They can be defined as either a limited set of possible values or an infinite set of possible values

3. When implementing an interface in a class:

    a. You can omit the public keyword as the field will be public by default

    b. You have to write the public keyword

Summary

In this chapter, we've learnt a lot of things about interfaces, typedefs, and enums.

Specifically, we covered how to write interfaces and what they can be used for. We've also defined what typedefs are and how they can be useful. We've seen how to declare and use enums with and without parameters and, at last, we've seen how to create iterable objects.

Now, you are ready to move to the next chapter to learn how to make several haXe applications communicate.

7
Communication Between haXe Programs

Using haXe remoting.

haXe is a language perfectly suited for web-applications. When one says web applications, it generally means connected applications. Fortunately, haXe has a system to help applications communicate: haXe remoting.

In this chapter, we will talk about haXe remoting and how it can be used to make our haXe applications communicate. As you will see, it is in fact pretty easy to use.

In this chapter, we will:

- ◆ Learn about the haXe serializer
- ◆ Use Neko and PHP applications as clients and servers
- ◆ Create a JS client
- ◆ Create a Flash client
- ◆ Communicate between Flash and JS

Although this is all pretty easy to do and understand, it is also very useful.

So, if you are ready, let's move on!

The haXe serializer

haXe has its own serializing system. This serializing system is the one used by haXe remoting therefore, before continuing with haXe remoting, it is important to understand how the haXe serializer works.

Usefulness

The haXe serializer is used by the haXe remoting system, but you can also use it on your own.

Doing so will allow you to get a string representation of almost any value. This way, you can, for example, store it on disk, in a database, or send it over any network connection.

Possibilities

The haXe serializer allows you to serialize almost any value, but still there are some things that you should know about how some values are serialized.

Basically, you should know that you can serialize:

- Ints
- Floats
- Bools
- Strings
- nulls
- haXe.io.Bytes
- Arrays
- List
- Hash
- Class instances
- Enum instances
- Anonymous objects
- Exceptions

Now, let's see what you need to know about how these are serialized.

Class instances

When you serialize a class instance, all of its fields are serialized and it also stores the class' name. When you want to unserialize the string, the unserializer will create an empty instance of the class without calling its constructor. It will then unserialize the fields' values and set the fields.

Note that for the unserialization to work, the application that consumes the serialized data must have the class definitions for all classes that are used in the serialized data.

However, since haXe 2.06, it is possible to use custom serialization.

Custom serialization

You can, in your own class, implement a specific way of serializing and unserializing it. To do so, you just need to implement the `hxSerialize` and `hxUnserialize` functions in your class.

Enum instances

Enum instances are serialized by storing the enum's name, the constructor's name, and its parameters.

The only limitation related to enums is that you cannot add or remove, or modify constructor's parameters.

Alternatively, as storing the constructor's name can take up quite a lot of space, you can tell the serializer to store the constructor's index instead. To do that, you can either set the static variable `haxe.Serializer.USE_ENUM_INDEX` to true, or just set the `useEnumIndex` field of an instance of `haxe.Serializer` to true.

If you do so, you will introduce a new constraint: you won't be able to change the order of your constructors. Just as it is for classes, the application that consumes the serialized data must have the enum defined.

Unserializing exceptions

If the value you are unserializing contains an exception, this exception will automatically be thrown.

This is something you should take into account: unserializing may throw an exception even though the unserializing in itself went well.

Reducing size and preventing infinite loops

If you are serializing data that can contain circular references (or that may contain several times the same data), then you should set `haxe.Serializer.USE_CACHE` to `true` (or an instance of `haxe.Serializer'suseCache` field to true).

This will slow things down a bit, but it may reduce the size of the serialized data by removing those that appear several times and will prevent infinite loops in case of circular references.

haXe remoting

The haXe remoting system can be used with all haXe's targets, but the functionalities which you will be able to use won't be the same as they vary/alter according to the type of platform used.

In addition, haXe remoting can be used over several protocols or transport layers. Again, the ability to use some of them will depend on the platform you are targeting.

Supported protocols and layers

As we discussed earlier, haXe remoting can be used on top of several protocols and transport layers. Functionalities and supported protocols depend on the target platform.

Here are the main supported protocols, by which class they are implemented, and an example of what they can be used for.

Over HTTP

It is possible to use haXe remoting over HTTP. This allows a client to query a server over the HTTP transport and has the advantage of being possible from most platforms.

It is possible to do so in both asynchronous and synchronous modes. In the first case, one will use the `haxe.remoting.HttpAsyncConnection` and in the later, `haxe.remoting.HttpConnection`.

On the server side, it is always the `haxe.remoting.HttpConnection` that will be used to implement your server to answer to those requests.

Note that using this connection, the requests can only go from the the client to the server, then the server will send its response. The server cannot initiate a request.

Implementation

On the client side, it is pretty simple—we just have to create our connection, give a URL pointing to our server, and then we can make requests.

```
class Client
{

    public static function main()
    {
        //The URL where our server is located
    var url = "http://localhost:8888/remoting/index.php";
        //Create the connection
    var cnx = haxe.remoting.HttpAsyncConnection.urlConnect(url);
        //Define a function to be called if an error arises.
    cnx.setErrorHandler(errorHandler);
        //Make the call.
    cnx.Server.add.call([1,2],displayResult);
    }

    /**
    *  This function is used as a callback to display the result
    */
    static function displayResult(result:Int)
    {
        trace(result);
    }

    public static function errorHandler(error)
    {
        trace("Error:" + error);
    }
}
```

On the server side, we will first have to create a context and add objects that clients should be able to access via this context:

```
#if neko
import neko.Lib;
#end
#if php
import php.Lib;
#end

class Server
{
```

```
public function new()
{
}

/**
 *  Clients will be able to call this function
 *  It simply returns the sum of two Int's
 */
public function add(x:Int,y:Int):Int
{
    return x + y;
}

public static function main()
{
    //Create a context
    var ctx = new haxe.remoting.Context();
    //Create an instance of server
    var server = new Server();
    //Add our instance of Server in the context
    //This way clients will be able to access it
    ctx.addObject("Server", server);
    //Handle the request
    if(haxe.remoting.HttpConnection.handleRequest(ctx))
        return;
    //If request couldn't be handled (i.e. if it was not a remoting
      request)
    //Print a message
    Lib.print("This is a remoting server.");
}
}
```

Using the ExternalInterface

The ExternalInterface is a way that is used by Flash to communicate with its hosting environment (which is, most of the time, the browser). Using this, Flash and JavaScript can communicate in the following ways:

 ♦ Flash can access variables from JavaScript

 ♦ Flash can call functions from JavaScript and get their return value

 ♦ Flash can share functions that JavaScript will be able to call

There is a limitation though: it is not possible to share DOM nodes through the ExternalInterface or AS3 classes' instances.

It is possible to use haXe remoting over the ExternalInterface. If you do that, you will be able to make calls from a Flash application embedded in a web page to some JavaScript code running in this web page. Calling from the JavaScript code to the Flash one will be possible too.

Now, let's see how we can implement this.

The JavaScript side

We are going to use `haxe.remoting.ExternalConnection` on both sides.

As you are going to see, it is pretty easy and works in the same way as it does over HTTP. However, there is a little thing we need to pay attention to—the Flash code has to be initialized and running before we can connect to it from JavaScript.

Therefore, to sum things up, we are going to create a context, add some object to it, and create our connection. To do so, we will use the `flashConnect` function from the `haxe. remoting.ExternalConnection` class and we will not only give it the context, but also a connection name and, more importantly, the ID of the Flash node in our HTML page.

```
class JSSide
{
    public static function substract(x:Int,y:Int):Int
    {
        return x - y;
    }

    public static function main()
    {
        //Create a context for objects we are going to share with Flash
    var ctx = new haxe.remoting.Context();
        //Add the current class to it (It will be able to access static
          vars and functions)
    ctx.addObject("JSCode",JSSide);
        //Create the connection
    var cnx = haxe.remoting.ExternalConnection.flashConnect
      ("default", "myFlashObject", ctx);
        //Make the call.
        trace(cnx.FlashCode.add.call([1,2]));
    }
}
```

As you can see, it is very simple.

In addition, this kind of connection works in a synchronous way, which is why we do not provide any callbacks.

The Flash side

On the Flash side, things are going to work the same way.

The main difference is that we are going to use the jsConnect function of the haxe. remoting.ExternalConnection class. We will provide it with the following two parameters:

1. The connection's name.
2. The context.

So, let's see some code:

```
class FlashSide
{
    public static function add(x:Int,y:Int):Int
    {
        return x + y;
    }

    public static function main()
    {
        //Create a context for objects we are going to share with Flash
    var ctx = new haxe.remoting.Context();
        //Add the current class to it (It will be able to access
            static vars and functions)
    ctx.addObject("FlashCode",FlashSide);
        //Create the connection
    var cnx = haxe.remoting.ExternalConnection.jsConnect
      ("default", ctx);
        //Make the call.
        trace(cnx.JSCode.substract.call([1,2]));
    }
}
```

As you can see, it is pretty simple and can be really useful. Often your solution will need several parts to work. Some projects, for example, use some AS2 code, some AS3 code, and some Javascript code—they can make everything communicate this way' to ensure grammatical sense and clarity.

Please, note that since ExternalInterface only works with Flash Player 8 and better, this connection can be used only on such players.

Using AMF

AMF is a protocol generally used with Flash when performing some remoting because it is natively implemented in the Flash player.

It is not really used by haXe remoting but haXe offers an interface that can be used like other haXe remoting interfaces and works with AMF services.

If you have a class `MyAFMService` with an `add` function in your AMF service, then you can use the following code to interact with it:

```
class AMFTest {

    public static function main()
    {
        var url = "http://localhost:8888/AMF/gateway.php";
        var cnx = haxe.remoting.AMFConnection.urlConnect(url);
        cnx.setErrorHandler(onError);
        cnx.MyAMFService.add.call([1,2],displayResult);
    }

    public static function displayResult(r:Dynamic)
    {
        trace("result:"+r);
    }

    public static function onError(e:Dynamic)
    {
        trace("error:"+Std.string(e));
    }

}
```

AMF connections are always asynchronous and it is not possible to create your AMF services as you would with other `haXeRemoting` interfaces.

In addition, note that enums and classes' instances cannot be sent using AMF; so, you should stick to basic types such as int, string, and so on.

Time for action – Writing a zoo management tool

To illustrate what we have learned in this chapter, we are going to write a very simple tool based on zoo management.

This tool will have a server on which the list of animals will be stored and that will execute clients' queries.

Therefore, the server will basically offer the following two methods:

1. The first one will return the list of animals.

2. The second one will allow creating and adding an animal in the list.

An animal will simply consist in a name and a number of this animal.

On the client side, we will create a neko application in command line that will simply offer the same two functionalities, but exposed for the user.

The Animal class

In order to store information about animals, we will create a class named `Animal`. This class will be very simple, but it will have to be shared by both the client and the server. Indeed, the server will serialize several instances of this class, which means that the client will need this class to be able to unserialize it.

So, let's see how this class looks:

```
package zooKeeper;

class Animal
{
    public var name : String;
    public var number : Int;

    public function new()
    {
        name = "";
        number = 0;
    }
}
```

Representing the zoo

On the server side, we will create a class named `Zoo`, which will hold the list of animals and will provide two methods to load and save this list onto disk.

Time for action – Saving the list

In order to save the list, we will serialize it and save the result in a file. This indeed is certainly not the best way to do things but in our case, it will be enough.

```
public static function save()
{
    php.io.File.putContent("zookeeper.data",
      haxe.Serializer.run(animals));
}
```

Very simple, isn't it? We are simply serializing the animals list and dumping the result directly in the `zookeeper.data` file.

Time for action – Loading the list

Loading the list is a bit more complicated; it is possible that the file does not exist and in this case, we just want to start with a new list.

Let's see how we can handle that:

```
public static function init()
{
    //Read the data from the zookeeper.data file
    try
    {
        animals = haxe.Unserializer.run(php.io.File.getContent
          ("zookeeper.data"));
    } catch(e:Dynamic)
    {
        //If reading from the file doesn't work
        //We can initialize a new list of animals
        animals = new List<Animal>();
    }
}
```

Ok, it is not so complicated in fact. We just had to wrap our reading with a `try` block. It could have been handled a bit better—we could have just had a look to see if the file existed. If it existed but the unserializing had failed, then it would mean that we have a true problem with the stored data.

So, here is our complete `Zoo` class:

```
package zooKeeper;

class Zoo
{
```

```
public static var animals : List<Animal>;

public static function init()
{
   //Read the data from the zookeeper.data file
   try
   {
      animals = haxe.Unserializer.run(php.io.File.getContent
         ("zookeeper.data"));
   } catch(e : Dynamic)
   {
      //If reading from the file doesn't work
      //We can initialize a new list of animals
      animals = new List<Animal>();
   }
}

public static function save()
{
   php.io.File.putContent("zookeeper.data",
      haxe.Serializer.run(animals));
}
}
```

The remoting service

We will now add our remoting service. This remoting service will provide clients with the following two methods:

1. `getList`: This method will return the list of animals.
2. `addAnimal`: This method will take a name and a number to create an animal and add it to the list of animals in the zoo.

In order to provide this service, we will simply create a class named `Service` and implement the preceding two functions in it.

The getList function

The `getList` function will simply return the list from the `Zoo` class:

```
public static function getList() : List<Animal>
{
   returnZoo.animals;
}
```

Ok, this one was pretty simple in our case.

The createAnimal function

The `addAnimal` method will create an instance of animal setting its name and number fields with the parameters it takes and adding it to the list of animals.

Here it is:

```
public static function createAnimal(name : String, quantity : Int)
{
    //Create a new Animal instance
    var a = new Animal();
    a.name = name;
    a.number = 0;
    //Add our newly created animal to the list
    Zoo.animals.add(a);
}
```

So, finally, here is our complete `Service` class:

```
package zooKeeper;

/**
 *  This class will be used as our Service
 */
class Service
{
    /**
     *  This function returns the list of Animals
     */
    public static function getList() : List<Animal>
    {
        returnZoo.animals;
    }

    /**
     *  This function allows one to add an animal to the Zoo
     */
    public static function createAnimal(name : String, quantity : Int)
    {
        //Create a new Animal instance
        var a = new Animal();
        a.name = name;
        a.number = 0;
        //Add our newly created animal to the list
        Zoo.animals.add(a);
    }
}
```

When you think that all of these functions will be called over the web and that their parameters and return values (even the list of instances of a class) will transit over the web too, it's really amazing to see how little work it is!

Tying it together

Now, we have to link all of these classes together to make our service live.

Let's see our main class:

```
class ZooKeeper
{

    public function new()
    {
    }

    public static function main(): Void
    {
        //Read the list of Animals from disk
        zooKeeper.Zoo.init();
        //Create the context
        var ctx = new haxe.remoting.Context();
        //Add our Service class to available objects
        ctx.addObject("Service", zooKeeper.Service);
        //Handle requests
        if(!haxe.remoting.HttpConnection.handleRequest(ctx))
        {
            //If not a Remoting request
            php.Lib.println("This is a remoting server only.");
        } else {
        //Save the list to disk
            zooKeeper.Zoo.save();
        }}
    }
}
```

That is it. Our service can now be compiled and put online.

The client

The client will be pretty easy to implement—it will simply display a menu with a list of actions. There will be only two:

◆ Display the list of animals

◆ Add an animal

As you have certainly guessed, for each action it will simply call the remoting server and display the result or take information from the user and pass it onto the server.

Time for action – Initializing the client connection

The first thing we need to do is to initialize our connection. We will store it in a static variable, as follows:

```
class ZooCommander
{
    public static var cnx : haxe.remoting.Connection;

    public static function main()
    {
        //Create the connection
        cnx = haxe.remoting.HttpConnection.urlConnect
           ("http://localhost:8888/ZooKeeper.phpdir/index.php");
    }
}
```

What just happened?

We have simply created a connection over HTTP to our server by passing its address as the parameter.

Now, let's create our two functions.

The createAnimal function

We will create a `createAnimal` function, which will be called by the main menu when the user chooses to add an animal to the list.

It will first ask for the required information and then make the request to the server:

```
public static function createAnimal()
{
    //Ask the user for the Animal's name
    neko.Lib.println("Enter animal's name");
    var name = neko.io.File.stdin().readLine();
    //Ask the user for the Animal's number
    neko.Lib.println("Enter animal's number");
    var number = Std.parseInt(neko.io.File.stdin().readLine());
    //Do request to server
    cnx.Service.createAnimal.call([name, number]);
}
```

The listAnimals function

The listAnimals function will also be called by the main menu when the user chooses to see which animals are in the zoo.

It will simply make a request to the server and then display the result:

```
public static function listAnimals()
{
    var animals : List<zooKeeper.Animal> =
        cnx.Service.getList.call([]);
    for(a in animals)
    {
        neko.Lib.println("Name:"+ a.name);
        neko.Lib.println("Number:"+ a.number);
        neko.Lib.println("----------");
    }
}
```

It is pretty simple.

The main menu

Now, let's create a basic main menu:

```
public static function mainMenu()
{
    var result : Int;
    do
    {
        Lib.println("ZooCommander:");
        Lib.println("1) Create an Animal.");
        Lib.println("2) List all Animals.");
        Lib.println("0) Exit");

        result = Std.parseInt(neko.io.File.stdin().readLine());
        switch(result)
        {
            case 1:
                createAnimal();
            case 2:
                listAnimals();
        }
    } while(result != 0);
}
```

So, our main class now looks like this:

```
importneko.Lib;

class ZooCommander
{
    public static var cnx : haxe.remoting.Connection;

    public static function main()
    {
        //Create the connection
        cnx = haxe.remoting.HttpConnection.urlConnect
            ("http://localhost:8888/ZooKeeper.phpdir/index.php");
        mainMenu();
    }

    public static function mainMenu()
    {
        var result : Int;
        do
        {
            Lib.println("ZooCommander:");
            Lib.println("1) Create an Animal.");
            Lib.println("2) List all Animals.");
            Lib.println("0) Exit");

            result = Std.parseInt(neko.io.File.stdin().readLine());
            switch(result)
            {
                case 1:
                    createAnimal();
                case 2:
                    listAnimals();
            }
        } while(result != 0);
    }

    public static function createAnimal()
    {
        //Ask the user for the Animal's name
        neko.Lib.println("Enter animal's name");
        var name = neko.io.File.stdin().readLine();
        //Ask the user for the Animal's number
        neko.Lib.println("Enter animal's number");
```

```
            var number = Std.parseInt(neko.io.File.stdin().readLine());
            //Do request to server
            cnx.Service.createAnimal.call([name, number]);
        }

    public static function listAnimals()
    {
        var animals : List<zooKeeper.Animal> =
            cnx.Service.getList.call([]);
        for(a in animals)
        {
            neko.Lib.println("Name:"+ a.name);
            neko.Lib.println("Number:"+ a.number);
            neko.Lib.println("----------");
        }
    }
}
```

That is it!

Compiling the client

Now, to compile your client, you have to make sure that the zooKeeper.Animal class is compiled in it. To do that, you simple have to add zooKeeper.Animal at the end of your command line to compile.

Now, you can run and use your program!

Have a go hero – Represent data from JS in Flash

Now, let's imagine that you want to draw a graph of 12 numerical values.

You have these values in your haXe code compiled to Javascript but you want the drawing to take place in Flash. You should find a way to pass the data from the Javascript side to the Flash one.

Pop quiz – Doing the things

1. The haXe remoting protocol uses:

    a. The haXe serializer

    b. The AMF protocol

    c. Its own custom protocol

2. Calls made using haXe remoting:

    a. Are made synchronously

    b. Are made asynchronously

    c. Can be made in both modes, depending on the used connection

Summary

In this chapter, we learned how you can make your haXe programs communicate together. Specifically, we covered how to communicate between Flash and JS, how to communicate across the network, and how the haXe serializer works.

In the next chapter, we will learn how to access databases.

8
Accessing Databases

Storing and accessing data.

Storing and accessing data in a database is an important part of programming. This is something which is often used in web and other developments.

When developing an application, whether it is a web application, a desktop application, or even a mobile application, we are dealing with a lot of data. Indeed, that's mostly why applications are around—dealing with data.

Using databases can help to make it easier to deal with data. They may help store and retrieve data, and moreover, they can help filter the data you are going to retrieve.

In this chapter, we will:

◆ Learn how to connect to MySQL databases

◆ Learn how to connect to SQLite databases

◆ See how to query databases

◆ See how to map haXe objects to databases

So now, if you're ready, let's go!

Connecting to databases

haXe offers you two connectors in its standard library. Those two connectors can be used when targeting the PHP or Neko platforms.

Unfortunately, at the time of writing, the standard library does not provide any way to connect to databases when targeting C++.

So, on PHP and Neko, you will be able to connect to MySQL and SQLite databases. Note that these two databases systems work by following two different schemes:

1. MySQL is based on a client/server model where your application is the client and connects to the server using a login and a password.

2. SQLite databases are stored in a file on your filesystem. Therefore, you will have to make sure that your user has the correct access rights on the file storing your database. SQLite databases are really good when you don't want to depend on installing and running a server. This is particularly interesting when you want to create some locally running applications.

php.db.Connection and neko.db.Connection

Whether we connect to a MySQL database or a SQLite one, what we are going to use in the end is an instance of the `php.db.Connection` class (or `neko.db.Connection` depending on the platform you are targeting).

These classes provide an abstraction layer—as all Relational Database Management Systems share several concepts, it is indeed possible to create such an abstraction layer.

So, the idea is simple: we are going to use a class specific to each database type to establish the connection, and the function we are going to use in this class will return a `php.db.Connection` instance (or `neko.db.Connection` instance if you're targeting Neko). This can be very useful if you plan to switch from one type of database to another one.

SQL usage

Unfortunately, even if most Relational Database Management Systems use SQL as a query language, they often implement it in slightly different ways.

Even if the haXe framework enables you to use `db.Connection` for all RDBMS, unfortunately that doesn't mean that if some parts of the SQL language are not implemented in the same way in different RDBMS, they will be unified. In fact, haXe doesn't really act as an abstraction layer over SQL. Still, it tries to provide some helpers to assist you with this.

We will now see what can be used.

The interface

So, let's see what the `php.db.Connection` and `neko.db.Connection` interfaces have to provide to help us.

The close function

This function allows you to close the connection to the database. This is the last function that you should call on your instance. Incidentally, remembering to close connections when you know you won't need them anymore is important because some servers may be limited by how many connections they can serve concurrently.

The commit function

Most RDBMS have a system made of committing and rolling back changes. This is why you can use the `commit` function.

The rollback function

Coming with the `commit` function is the `rollback` function. It allows you to rollback the changes that you have not committed yet.

The escape function

The `escape` function takes a string as a parameter and escapes it according to what the RDBMS you are connected to requires. This should be used in order to help prevent SQL-injection.

This function also returns the escaped string.

The quote function

The `quote` function does the same thing as the `escape` function although it will also add quotes (or the correct characters to delimit strings in the RDBMS you are connected to).

This function returns the corresponding string.

The request function

The `request` function allows one to send a query to the server and receive a result.

Your request should be sent as a string in any language which the server you are connected to can understand (that is usually SQL).

If your query returns any result, then you will get it through a `ResultSet` that will be returned by the function.

We will see later how you can deal with results.

The addValue function

This function takes a `StringBuf` and any value as parameters. It adds the correct representation (as expected by the server you are connected to) of the value to the `StringBuf`.

This function returns nothing as the `StringBuf` is directly modified.

The dbName function

This function simply returns the name of the database you are working on at the moment. It doesn't allow you to change it.

The lastInsertId function

This function is a very useful one. When you insert a new record in the database, this function will allow you to retrieve the ID of the last inserted record.

You will certainly need it if you leave it up to the server to automatically generate the ID of the record.

This function returns an `int`.

Connecting to the database

Connecting to the database will depend on which RDBMS you are trying to connect to. Let's see how this can be done for the two RDBMS that are supported at the moment.

MySQL

Connecting to MySQL is done by calling the `php.db.Mysql.connect` (or `neko.db.Mysql.connect`) function and passing its connection information through an anonymous object.

```
class HxDatabase
{
    public static function main(): Void
    {
        var connection : neko.db.Connection;

        var options =   {
                    user : "myUserName",
                    pass : "myPassword",
                    socket : null,
                    host : "localhost",
                    port : 3306,
                    database : "MyBase"
            };
        connection = neko.db.Mysql.connect(options);
        //Do things with the database
        //Do not forget to close the connection
        connection.close();
    }
}
```

Let's see the different options given to the function:

- ◆ user: This simply is a string with your username
- ◆ pass: This is a string with your password
- ◆ socket: If you are connecting through a local socket instead of connecting through TCP/IP, then provide its path here
- ◆ host: This is the host to connect to
- ◆ port: This is the server's port to connect to and should be given as an int
- ◆ database: This is the name of the database to use

This is pretty easy indeed.

SQLite

Using SQLite databases is even simpler—you will only need to pass the path to the database's file to the neko.db.Sqlite.open function. If the current user has the correct rights on the file on the filesystem, then everything should be fine.

```
class HxDatabase
{
    public static function main(): Void
    {
        var connection : neko.db.Connection;

        connection = neko.db.Sqlite.open("test.db");
        connection.close();
    }
}
```

It is that simple.

Dealing with results

When you are executing a request, it will eventually return a ResultSet. Using such results is quite easy:

```
class HxDatabase
{
    public static function main(): Void
    {
        var connection : neko.db.Connection;

        var options =   {
                        user : "myUserName",
```

```
                        pass : "myPassword",
                        socket : null,
                        host : "localhost",
                        port : 3306,
                        database : "MyBase"
            };
        neko.db.Mysql.connect(options);

        //Query and store results
        var results = connection.request("SELECT * FROM users;");

        //Iterate over each result
        for(res in results)
        {
            neko.Lib.println("User " + res.name + " is aged " res.age);
        }

        connection.close();
    }
}
```

You can note two things:

1. We can iterate over a `ResultSet` to get all results as a Dynamic object.
2. We can use the field's name as a field on the result object.

If the fields you want to access do not have any names, then you can access them using the `getFloatResult`, `getIntResult`, and `getResult` functions. They all expect an `int` as a parameter to know the index of the field you want to access (starting at 0).

Typing

You may wonder what the types of objects are when you access them through the field's name. Well, for MySQL, there is a simple table showing the correspondence between the SQL type and the haXe type:

MySQL	haXe
DATE	Date
DATETIME	Date
TINYINT	Short
SHORT	Int
INT24	Int
LONG	Int
LONGLONG	Float

MySQL	haXe
DECIMAL	Float
FLOAT	Float
DOUBLE	Float
TINYINT(1)	Bool
BLOB	String

All other types are converted to string.

The SPOD

SPOD stands for **Simple Persistence Objects Database**. It is a functionality of the library to allow one to define objects in haXe and save and retrieve them easily from a database.

In fact, you will need to map haXe classes to tables in your database and you will be able to insert new records, delete them, update them, and search them.

Setting a SPOD object

To create objects that you will be able to use as SPOD objects, you have to create a class that extends `neko.db.Object` or `php.db.Object`.

Simply create the fields that exist in your table in the class as you would normally do:

```
class User extends neko.db.Object
{
    public var id : Int;
    public var userName : String;
    public var password : String;
}
```

We will also need to define a `manager`; it will be in charge of managing many operations for objects of this type. There is a standard one that you can use:

```
class User extends neko.db.Object
{
    public var id : Int;
    public var userName : String;
    public var password : String;

    public static var manager = new neko.db.Manager<User>(User);
}
```

Note that if you share the same class across, for example, Neko and Flash because of remoting, you may want to use conditional compilation:

```
class User #if neko extends neko.db.Object #end
{
   public var id : Int;
   public var userName : String;
   public var password : String;

   #ifneko public static var manager = new neko.
     db.Manager<User>(User); #end
}
```

The table name

By default, objects will be mapped to a table that has the same name as the classes.

Should you want to change the table's name that is used; you can do so by defining the static variable such as TABLE_NAME:

```
class User extends neko.db.Object
{
   public var id : Int;
   public var userName : String;
   public var password : String;

   private static var TABLE_NAME = "Users"; //Will use the table
     Users instead of User
   public static var manager = new neko.db.Manager<User>(User);
}
```

> **Note:** You should always define the manager as the last variable. By doing this, you can be sure that all other static variables will be initialized before the manager. This is important because the manager will use some of them for configuration.

Non-mapped fields

You may want to have some fields in your haXe class although they won't be present in the database. This is perfectly possible and is sometime useful.

To do so, simply create a static variable named `PRIVATE_FIELDS`; it has to be an array of string containing every field's name that you do not want to see mapped to the database:

```
class User extends neko.db.Object
{
   public var id : Int;
   public var userName : String;
   public var password : String;
   public var helper : String;

   private static var TABLE_NAME = "Users"; //Will use the table
     Users instead of User
   private static var PRIVATE_FIELDS = ["helper"];
   public static var manager = new neko.db.Manager<User>(User);
}
```

In this example, the field `helper` won't be mapped to anything in the database. This can be used, for example, when you have queries that join tables.

The cache

There is a cache system implemented in the library and all objects retrieved from the database are stored in it.

The goal behind this system is to make sure that even if you have several references to the same object in a database (several objects with the same ID and from the same table), whenever you make a change to any of its field, it's replicated to all references of this object.

There is a way to clear the cache; you simply have to call the `neko.db.Manager.cleanup` or the `php.db.Manager.cleanup` function.

A concrete example of SPOD use

Let's see a concrete example of how to use that.

Set up a database in your MySQL server with a table named `Users`.

In this table, add the following three fields:

1. `id`: This should be the Primary Key and have `auto_increment`, so that we don't have to worry about generating the Primary Keys.
2. `username`: This should be a text; we will use it to store the user's username.
3. `password`: This should be a text too; we will use it to store the user's password hash.

Setting the object

Now, let's create a `User` class reflecting those fields and useable as SPOD:

```
class User extends neko.db.Object
{
   public var id : Int;
   public var username : String;
   public var password : String;

   public static var manager = new neko.db.Manager<User>(User);
}
```

 Note: We are going to use the standard `Manager`.

Remember how we named our table `Users` and see how our class is named `User`? This makes perfect sense and it respects/accounts for what people are used to seeing. Still, we will need to tell the `manager` to use the `Users` table and not the `User` one. Therefore, let's just add our `TABLE_NAME` static variable as follows:

```
class User extends neko.db.Object
{
   public var id : Int;
   public var username : String;
   public var password : String;

   private static var TABLE_NAME = "Users";
   public static var manager = new neko.db.Manager<User>(User);
}
```

Now, let's see how to integrate this in an application.

Setting the connection

In our `main` function, let's initiate a connection to our database as follows:

```
class HxDatabase
{
   public static function main(): Void
   {
      var connection : neko.db.Connection;

      var options =    {
                        user : "myUserName",
```

```
                    pass : "myPassword",
                    socket : null,
                    host : "localhost",
                    port : 3306,
                    database : "MyBase"
            };
        connection = neko.db.Mysql.connect(options);

    }
}
```

This is good, but not enough. We have to tell the `neko.db.Manager` or `php.db.Manager` class to use this connection to work; this is done by setting the `cnx` property on it as shown in the following code snippet:

```
class HxDatabase
{
    public static function main(): Void
    {
        var connection : neko.db.Connection;

        var options =   {
                        user : "myUserName",
                        pass : "myPassword",
                        socket : null,
                        host : "localhost",
                        port : 3306,
                        database : "MyBase"
            };
        connection = neko.db.Mysql.connect(options);
        //Tell manager to use this connection.
        neko.db.Manager.cnx = connection;

    }
}
```

Now, let's list all our registered users as follows:

```
class HxDatabase
{
    public static function main(): Void
    {
        var connection : neko.db.Connection;

        var options =   {
```

```
                        user  :  "myUserName",
                        pass  :  "myPassword",
                        socket  :  null,
                        host  :  "localhost",
                        port  :  3306,
                        database  :  "MyBase"
            };
        connection = neko.db.Mysql.connect(options);
        //Tell manager to use this connection.
        neko.db.Manager.cnx = connection;
        neko.db.Manager.initialize();

        //Get list of all users (not locking them)
        var users = User.manager.all(false);
        for(user in users)
        {
            neko.Lib.print("User:"+user.username);
        }

        //Close connection
        connection.close();
    }
}
```

Don't worry, we are going to have a look at what the Manager class has to offer, but as you can already see, it offers the `all` function that returns a list of our objects. This is why we get a list of users here.

The Manager

We have already seen how to initialize the manager, now, let's have a quick look at what it has to offer.

The all function

This function returns a list of all records present in the table. It takes an optional lock parameter that, if true, indicates that records that are going to be retrieved should have a lock put on them.

The count function

This function allows you to get the number of records that are present in the table. It can take an optional anonymous object as a parameter in order to filter records. By doing this, you can, for example, pass this object {sex : "M"} if you want to get only records corresponding to a male person.

The delete function

The delete function allows you to delete objects. Just like the count function, it can take an anonymous object to filter records that will be concerned.

The get function

The get function is certainly one of the most important functions; it allows you to retrieve an object from the database based on its Primary Key. It can also get an optional lock parameter similar to the all function.

The getWithKeys function

This function allows you to retrieve objects with several keys; it takes an optional anonymous object to specify keys and their values, and an optional lock parameter.

The object function

This function takes a String as a parameter that has to be a SQL request. It then returns an object representing a result from the database. This function can also take an optional lock parameter.

The objects function

This functions works in the same way as the object function, the difference is that it will return a list of objects.

The search function

This function allows you to retrieve some objects by filtering them through an anonymous object. It also takes an optional lock parameter.

There are some other functions available but enumerating them here would not be of any interest. You can have a look at the API at the following URL:

```
http://www.haxe.org/api
```

Handling relations

Most of the time, you have modeled your database with relations inside it.

The haXe SPOD is able to handle one-to-one and many-to-one relations.

This is done by implementing the static function RELATIONS that takes no parameter. It has to return an array of anonymous objects made of the fields prop, key, and manager.

The prop field will be a string that is the name of a property by which you will get and set the object. This property has to be a dynamic property.

The key field is also a string that is the name of the field (in the database) that stores the foreign key.

So, let's take our User example and a sponsorship program to it. A user can sponsor another one.

```
class User extends neko.db.Object
{
    public var id : Int;
    public var username : String;
    public var password : String;
    public var sponsorId : Int; //Foreign Key
    //The property
    public var sponsor(dynamic, dynamic) : User;
    //Our function
    static function RELATIONS()
    {
        return [{prop: "sponsor", key: "sponsorId", manager:
          User.manager}];
    }

    private static var TABLE_NAME = "Users";
    public static var manager = new neko.db.Manager<User>(User);
}
```

As you can see, sponsorId is our Foreign Key (it has to be a field in your table). When you want a user to sponsor another user, you will have to use the sponsor property.

Creating a blogging system

Now that we have seen how we can query databases and how we can use the SPOD system, we are going to try implementing something that looks like a very simple blogging system.

We will have the following four functionalities:

1. Adding a new post.
2. Listing posts.
3. Adding a user.
4. Listing users.

In order to choose what actions we want to execute, we will use the GET parameter "action". We will also pass other parameters needed by the action through GET parameters.

Time for action – Creating the Users table

Firstly, we are going to create a table named Users which will hold information about users. We will need the following three fields:

1. username: Will hold the user's login.
2. password: Will hold the user's password hashed.
3. id: The Primary Key.

The following is the SQL query you can use to create this table:

```
CREATE TABLE 'Users' (
  'id' int(11) NOT NULL AUTO_INCREMENT,
  'username' varchar(255) NOT NULL,
  'password' varchar(255) NOT NULL,
  PRIMARY KEY ('id')
) ENGINE=MyISAM  DEFAULT CHARSET=utf8;
```

What just happened?

This will create the table and the ID will also have auto_increment set on it.

Time for action – Creating the User class

Now, we will create the User class that maps to the Users table as follows:

```
package hxBlog;

#ifneko
import neko.db.Object;
import neko.db.Manager;
#end

#ifphp
import php.db.Object;
import php.db.Manager;
#end


class User extends Object
{
   public var id : Int;
   public var username : String;
   public var password : String;

   static var TABLE_NAME = "Users";
   public static var manager = new Manager<User>(User);

   public function setPassword(password : String)
   {
      this.password = haxe.Md5.encode(password);
   }
}
```

What just happened?

There are several things to note here:

◆ We are redefining the table to use by setting the TABLE_NAME static variable to Users

◆ We have created a simple function to set the password to the hash of the password

◆ We are performing some imports depending on the platform, so that our application can run in both Neko and PHP

Time for action – Creating the Posts table

We will now create a table named `Posts` which will hold all our blog posts.

This table will have the following five fields:

1. `id`: The ID of the post
2. `title`: The post's title
3. `body`: The post's text
4. `fk_author`: This will contain the ID of the author
5. `postedOn`: The date when the post was published

The following is the SQL query that you can use to create this table:

```
CREATE TABLE 'Posts' (
  'id' int(11) NOT NULL AUTO_INCREMENT,
  'title' text NOT NULL,
  'body' longtext NOT NULL,
  'fk_author' int(11) NOT NULL,
  'postedOn' datetime NOT NULL,
  PRIMARY KEY ('id')
) ENGINE=MyISAM  DEFAULT CHARSET=utf8;
```

Our table will be set correctly with this query.

Time for action – Creating the Post class

We will now create the `Post` class mapping to the `Posts` table.

We will need to redefine the table it is mapped to.

We will also need to define its relation to the User table.

```
package hxBlog;

#ifneko
import neko.db.Object;
import neko.db.Manager;
#end

#ifphp
import php.db.Object;
import php.db.Manager;
#end
```

```
class Post extends Object
{
   public var id : Int;
   public var title : String;
   public var body : String;
   public var postedOn : Date;
   public var fk_author : Int;

   public var author(dynamic, dynamic) : hxBlog.User;

   static function RELATIONS()
   {
      return [{prop: "author", key: "fk_author", manager:
         User.manager}];
   }

   static var TABLE_NAME = "Posts";
   public static var manager = new Manager<Post>(Post);
}
```

What just happened?

As you can see, we have our imports at the top of the class to ensure that this will work on Neko and PHP.

We also have the fk_author field definition and most importantly, we have the author property that is used in the RELATIONS static function.

This relation will use author as the property and fk_author as the field that holds the key. Finally, the manager is the one of the User class because it is linked to the Users table.

Time for action – Creating the connection to the database

For our main function, we are going to do it systematically.

At first, let's create the connection to the database:

```
#if neko
import neko.db.Connection;
import neko.db.Mysql;
import neko.db.Manager;
import neko.Web;
import neko.Lib;
#end
```

```
#ifphp
import php.db.Connection;
import php.db.Mysql;
import php.db.Manager;
import php.Web;
import php.Lib;
#end

class HxBlog
{
   public static function main(): Void
   {
      var connection : Connection;

      var options =    {
                     user : "root",
                     pass : "root",
                     socket : null,
                     host : "127.0.0.1",
                     port : 8889,
                     database : "hxBlog"
            };
      connection = Mysql.connect(options);
      //Tell manager to use this connection.
      Manager.cnx = connection;
      Manager.initialize();

      //Do things

      connection.close();
   }
}
```

What just happened?

This just sets things, so that we have everything set to work on both the PHP and Neko targets.

In addition, it will connect to the local server, on port 8889 and will use the hxBlog database.

Time for action – Listing posts

Now, let's create a function to list posts. This one is pretty easy:

```
public static function listPosts()
{
    Lib.println("Listing posts:<br/>");
    for(p in hxBlog.Post.manager.all(false))
    {
        Lib.print(p.title+"(posted on"+p.postedOn.toString() +
            "by"+p.author.username+")<br/>");
        Lib.print(p.body+"<br/>");
    }
}
```

As you can see, it simply prints information from every post.

Also, note that you can use the `User` object corresponding to the `author` directly. This is one of the most interesting parts of the SPOD system.

Therefore, our `main` class now looks like this:

```
#ifneko
import neko.db.Connection;
import neko.db.Mysql;
import neko.db.Manager;
import neko.Web;
import neko.Lib;
#end

#ifphp
import php.db.Connection;
import php.db.Mysql;
import php.db.Manager;
import php.Web;
import php.Lib;
#end

class HxBlog
{
    public static function main(): Void
    {
        var connection : Connection;

        var options =    {
```

```
                    user : "root",
                    pass : "root",
                    socket : null,
                    host : "127.0.0.1",
                    port : 8889,
                    database : "hxBlog"
            };
        connection = Mysql.connect(options);
        //Tell manager to use this connection.
        Manager.cnx = connection;
        Manager.initialize();

        //Do things

        connection.close();
    }

    public static function listPosts()
    {
        Lib.println("Listing posts:<br/>");
        for(p in hxBlog.Post.manager.all(false))
        {
            Lib.print(p.title+"(posted on"+p.postedOn.toString()+
                "by"+p.author.username+")<br/>");
            Lib.print(p.body+"<br/>");
        }
    }
}
```

Time for action – Listing users

Now, we are going to create a function to list all users.

This one is even simpler than listing posts because it has no relations.

```
    public static function listUsers()
    {
        Lib.print("Users:<br/>");
        for(u in hxBlog.User.manager.all(false))
        {
            Lib.print(u.username+"<br/>");
        }
    }
```

Our class now looks like the following:

```
#ifneko
import neko.db.Connection;
import neko.db.Mysql;
import neko.db.Manager;
import neko.Web;
import neko.Lib;
#end

#ifphp
import php.db.Connection;
import php.db.Mysql;
import php.db.Manager;
import php.Web;
import php.Lib;
#end

class HxBlog
{
    public static function main(): Void
    {
        var connection : Connection;

        var options =    {
                    user : "root",
                    pass : "root",
                    socket : null,
                    host : "127.0.0.1",
                    port : 8889,
                    database : "hxBlog"
            };
        connection = Mysql.connect(options);
        //Tell manager to use this connection.
        Manager.cnx = connection;
        Manager.initialize();

        //Do things

        connection.close();
    }

    public static function listPosts()
    {
```

```
Lib.println("Listing posts:<br/>");
for(p in hxBlog.Post.manager.all(false))
{
    Lib.print(p.title+"(posted on"+p.postedOn.toString()+
        "by"+p.author.username+")<br/>");
    Lib.print(p.body+"<br/>");
}
}

public static function listUsers()
{
    Lib.print("Users:<br/>");
    for(u in hxBlog.User.manager.all(false))
    {
        Lib.print(u.username+"<br/>");
    }
}
}
```

Time for action – Adding a user

Now, let's create the function to add a user. It will take the login and the password as
parameters and will return the created object as follows:

```
public static function createUser(login : String, password :
    String) : hxBlog.User
{

    var u = new hxBlog.User();
    u.username = login;
    u.setPassword(password);
    u.insert();
    return u;
}
```

Time for action – Adding a post

The function to create a post will have a little twist because it will have to set the author of
the post. It will take, among other information, the name of the author. We will then retrieve
the author's object by using the manager's search function.

```
public static function createPost(authorLogin : String, title :
    String, body : String) : hxBlog.Post
{
    var author = hxBlog.User.manager.search({username :
        authorLogin}, false).first();
```

```
      var p = new hxBlog.Post();
      p.author = author;
      p.title = title;
      p.body = body;
      p.postedOn = Date.now();
      p.insert();
      return p;
}
```

Time for action – Branching it with the main function

Now, let's just add some code to act depending on the action GET parameters and get all parameters as needed by the action and pass them to our functions:

```
//Depending on the action GET parameter to do things:
switch(Web.getParams().get("action"))
{
   case "listPosts":
      listPosts();
   case "addUser":
      createUser(Web.getParams().get("login"),
        Web.getParams().get("password"));
   case "listUsers":
      listUsers();
   case "addPost":
      createPost(Web.getParams().get("author"),
        Web.getParams().get("title"), Web.getParams().get("body"));
   default:
      listPosts();
}
```

Therefore, our complete class is as follows:

```
#if neko
import neko.db.Connection;
import neko.db.Mysql;
import neko.db.Manager;
import neko.Web;
import neko.Lib;
#end

#if php
import php.db.Connection;
import php.db.Mysql;
import php.db.Manager;
```

```
import php.Web;
import php.Lib;
#end

class HxBlog
{
  public static function main(): Void
  {
    var connection : Connection;

    var options =    {
                  user : "root",
                  pass : "root",
                  socket : null,
                  host : "127.0.0.1",
                  port : 8889,
                  database : "hxBlog"
              };
    connection = Mysql.connect(options);
    //Tell manager to use this connection.
    Manager.cnx = connection;
    Manager.initialize();

    //Do things
    //Depending on the action GET parameter to do things:
    switch(Web.getParams().get("action"))
    {
      case "listPosts":
        listPosts();
      case "addUser":
        createUser(Web.getParams().get("login"),
          Web.getParams().get("password"));
      case "listUsers":
        listUsers();
      case "addPost":
        createPost(Web.getParams().get("author"),
          Web.getParams().get("title"),
          Web.getParams().get("body"));
      default:
        listPosts();
    }

    connection.close();
  }
```

```
    public static function listPosts()
    {
       Lib.println("Listing posts:<br/>");
       for(p in hxBlog.Post.manager.all(false))
       {
          Lib.print(p.title+"(posted on"+p.postedOn.toString()+
            "by"+p.author.username+")<br/>");
          Lib.print(p.body + "<br/>");
       }
    }

    public static function listUsers()
    {
       Lib.print("Users:<br/>");
       for(u in hxBlog.User.manager.all(false))
       {
          Lib.print(u.username+"<br/>");
       }
    }

    public static function createUser(login : String, password :
      String) : hxBlog.User
    {
       var u = new hxBlog.User();
       u.username = login;
       u.setPassword(password);
       u.insert();
       return u;
    }

    public static function createPost(authorLogin : String, title :
      String, body : String) : hxBlog.Post
    {
       var author = hxBlog.User.manager.search({username :
         authorLogin}, false).first();
       var p = new hxBlog.Post();
       p.author = author;
       p.title = title;
       p.body = body;
       p.postedOn = Date.now();
       p.insert();
       return p;
    }
  }
```

It's not that complicated, right?

Have a go hero – Listing posts from a specific user

Try to extend the preceding example, so that it is possible to easily list posts from a specific user by the user's name.

Pop quiz – Doing the things

1. It is possible to define fields that do not appear in the database by using:

    a. A static variable PRIVATE_FIELDS

    b. An instance variable PRIVATE_FIELDS

    c. A static variable NO_DB_FIELDS

2. The SPOD object does not know how to handle DATE fields from the MySQL database:

    a. True

    b. False

Summary

So, in this chapter, we have learned quite a lot of things about how to manipulate data from databases with haXe.

Specifically, we covered how to connect to MySQL and SQLite databases, how to query those databases with the low-level API, and how to use the SPOD library in order to store, retrieve, modify, and delete objects from the database.

Now that we know how to use databases, we will learn how we can do some templating. That may prove to be useful to display our objects in a more elegant way. So, are you ready? Let's go on!

9
Templating

Using templates.

Templates are a very useful feature of haXe. They help the developer with his job of presenting data to the user by making it easy to repeat some parts of a view (or page) and by allowing some branching depending on data.

As developers our job is to create programs that allow the manipulation of data. That's the basis of our job, but beyond this part of the job, we must also be able to present that data to the user. Programs that don't have a user interface exist, but since you are reading this book about haXe, there is a greater chance that you are mostly interested in web applications, and almost all web applications have a User Interface of some kind. However, these can also be used to create XML documents for example.

In this chapter, we will cover templating by talking about:

◆ The included `haxe.Template` class

◆ The syntax used by the templating system

◆ How data is passed to the templating system

◆ How a template can execute some actions

So if you are ready, let's go!

Introduction to the haxe.Template class

The haXe library comes with the `haxe.Template` class. This class allows for basic, yet quite powerful, templating: as we will see, it is not only possible to pass some data to it, but also possible to call some code from a template.

Templates are particularly useful when you have to present data—in fact, you can, for example, define a template to display data about a user and then iterate over a list of users displaying this template for each one.

We will see how this is possible during this chapter and we will see what else you can do with templates. We will also see that it is possible to change what is displayed depending on the data and also that it is easy to do some quite common things such as having a different style for one row out of two in a table.

The `haxe.Template` is really easy to use—you just have to create an instance of it passing it a String that contains your template's code as a parameter. Then it is as easy as calling the execute method and giving it some data to display.

Let's see a simple example:

```
class TestTemplate
{
    public static function main(): Void
    {
        var myTemplate = new haxe.Template("Hi. ::user::");
        neko.Lib.println(myTemplate.execute({user : "Benjamin"}));
    }
}
```

This simple code will output "Hi. Benjamin". This is because we have passed an anonymous object as a context with a "user" property that has "Benjamin" as value.

Obviously, you can pass objects with several properties. Moreover, as we will see it is even possible to pass complex structures and use them.

In addition, we certainly won't be hard coding our templates into our haXe code. Most of the time, you will want to load them from a resource compiled into your executable by calling `haxe.Resource.getString` or by directly loading them from the filesystem or from a database.

Printing a value

As we've seen in the preceding sample, we have to surround an expression with : : in order to print its value.

Expressions can be of several forms:

Form	Explanation
`::variableName::`	The value of the variable.
`::(123)::`	The integer 123. Note that only integers are allowed.
`::e1 operator e2::`	Applies the operator to e1 and e2 and returns the resulting value.
	The syntax doesn't manage operator precedence, so you should wrap expressions inside parenthesis.
`::e.field::`	Accesses the field and returns the value.
	Be warned that this doesn't work with properties' getters and setters as these properties are a compile-time only feature.

Branching

The syntax offers the `if`, `else`, and `elseif`:

```
class TestTemplate
{
    public static function main(): Void
    {
        var templateCode = "::if (sex==0):: Male ::elseif (sex==1)::
            Female ::else:: Unknown ::end::";
        var myTemplate = new haxe.Template(templateCode);
        neko.Lib.print(myTemplate.execute({user : "Benjamin", sex:0}));
    }
}
```

Here the output will be `Male`. But if the sex property of the context was set to 1 it would print `Female`, if it is something else, it will print "Unknown".

Note that our keywords are surrounded by `::` (so the interpreter won't think that it is just some raw-text to be printed).

Also note that the "end" keyword has been introduced since we do not use braces.

Using lists, arrays, and other iterables

The template engine allows one to iterate over an iterable and repeat a part of the template for each object in the iterable.

This is done using the `::foreach::` keyword. When iterating, the context will be modified and will become the object that is actually selected in the iterable.

It is also possible to access this object (indeed, the context's value) by using the `__current__` variable.

Let's see an example:

```
class Main
{
    public static function main()
    {
        //Let's create two departments:
        var itDep = new Department("Information Technologies Dept.");
        var financeDep = new Department("Finance Dept.");

        //Create some users and add them to their department
        var it1 = new Person();
        it1.lastName = "Par";
        it1.firstName = "John";
        it1.age = 22;

        var it2 = new Person();
        it2.lastName = "Bear";
        it2.firstName = "Caroline";
        it2.age = 40;

        itDep.workers.add(it1);
        itDep.workers.add(it2);

        var fin1 = new Person();
        fin1.lastName = "Ha";
        fin1.firstName = "Trevis";
        fin1.age = 43;

        var fin2 = new Person();
        fin2.lastName = "Camille";
        fin2.firstName = "Unprobable";
        fin2.age = 70;

        financeDep.workers.add(fin1);
        financeDep.workers.add(fin2);

        //Put our departements inside a List:
        var depts = new List<Department>();
        depts.add(itDep);
        depts.add(financeDep);
```

```
        //Load our template from Resource:
        var templateCode = haxe.Resource.getString("DeptsList");
        //Execute it
        var template = new haxe.Template(templateCode);
        neko.Lib.print(template.execute({depts: depts}));
    }
}

class Person
{
    public var lastName : String;
    public var firstName : String;
    public var age : Int;

    public function new()
    {

    }
}

class Department
{
    public var name : String;
    public var workers : List<Person>;

    public function new(name : String)
    {
        workers = new List<Person>();
        this.name = name;
    }
}
```

In this part of the code we are simply creating two departments, some persons, and adding those persons into those departments.

Now, we want to display the list of departments and all of the employees that work in them. So, let's write a simple template (you can save this file as `DeptsList.template`):

```
<html>
    <head>
        <title>Workers</title>    </head>
    <body>
        ::foreach depts::
        <h1>::name::</h1>
        <table>
```

```
        ::foreach workers::
        <tr>
           <td>::firstName::</td>
           <td>::lastName::</td>
           <td>::if (age < 35)::Junior::elseif (58):
              :Senior::else::Retired::end::</td>
        </tr>
        ::end::
     </table>
     ::end::
  </body>
</html>
```

When compiling your code you should add the following directive:

```
-resource DeptsList.template@DeptsList
```

This is to embed the file in our compiled code and make it available under the "DeptsList" name.

The following is the output you will get:

```
<html>
  <head>
     <title>Workers</title>   </head>
  <body>

     <h1>Information Technologies Dept.</h1>
     <table>

        <tr>
           <td>John</td>
           <td>Par</td>
           <td>Junior</td>
        </tr>

        <tr>
           <td>Caroline</td>
           <td>Bear</td>
           <td>F</td>
        </tr>

     </table>

     <h1>Finance Dept.</h1>
     <table>
```

```
    <tr>
        <td>Trevis</td>
        <td>Ha</td>
        <td>Senior</td>
    </tr>

    <tr>
        <td>Unprobable</td>
        <td>Camille</td>
        <td>Retired</td>
    </tr>

    </table>

    </body>
</html>
```

As you can see, this is indeed pretty simple once you have your data structure in place.

Time for action – Executing code from a template

Even though templates can't contain haXe code, they can make calls to so-called "template macros". Macros are defined by the developer and, just like data they are passed to the `template.execute` function. In fact, they are passed exactly in the same way, but as the second parameter.

Calling them is quite easy, instead of surrounding them with `: :` we will simply prefix them with `$$`, we can also pass them as parameters inside parenthesis. So, let's take our preceding sample and add a macro to display the number of workers in a department.

First, let's add the function to our `Main` class:

```
public static function displayNumberOfWorkers(resolve :
    String->Dynamic, department : Department)
{
    return department.workers.length + " workers";
}
```

Note that the first argument that the macro will receive is a function that takes a `String` and returns a `Dynamic`. This function will allow you to retrieve the value of an expression in the context from which the macro has been called.

Then, other parameters are simply the parameters that the template passes to the macro. So, let's add a call to our macro:

```
<html>
  <head>
  </head>
  <body>
    ::foreach depts::
    <h1>::name:: ($$displayNumberOfWorkers(::__current__::))</h1>
    <table>
      ::foreach workers::
      <tr>
         <td>::firstName::</td>
         <td>::lastName::</td>
         <td>::if (sex==0)::M::elseif (sex==1)::F::else::?::end::</td>
      </tr>
      ::end::
    </table>
    ::end::
  </body>
</html>
```

As you can see, we will pass the current department to the macro when calling it to display the number of workers.

So, here is what you get:

```
<html>
    <head>
    </head>
    <body>

        <h1>Information Technologies Dept. (2 workers)</h1>
        <table>

            <tr>
                <td>John</td>
                <td>Par</td>
                <td>M</td>
            </tr>

            <tr>
                <td>Caroline</td>
                <td>Bear</td>
```

```
            <td>F</td>
        </tr>

    </table>

    <h1>Finance Dept. (2 workers)</h1>
    <table>

        <tr>
            <td>Trevis</td>
            <td>Ha</td>
            <td>M</td>
        </tr>

        <tr>
            <td>Unprobable</td>
            <td>Camille</td>
            <td>?</td>
        </tr>

    </table>

    </body>
</html>
```

What just happened?

We have written the `displayNumberOfWorkers` macro and added a call to it in the template. As a result, we've been able to display the number of workers in a department.

Integrating subtemplates

Sub-templates do not exist as such in the templating system.

The fact is that you can include sub-templates into a main template, which is not a rare process. Some frameworks, not only in haXe, have even made this standard behavior.

So, there are two ways of doing this:

1. Execute the sub-template, store its return value, and pass it as a property to the main template when executing it.

2. Create a macro to execute the sub-template and return its value. This way you just have to call the macro whenever you want to include your sub-template in your main template.

Creating a blog's front page

In this section, we are going to create a front page for a blog by using the `haxe.Template` class.

We will also use the SPOD system to retrieve posts from the database.

Time for action – Creating our SPOD class

First, let's create a very simple SPOD class representing our blog posts.

Add this code to `Post.hx`:

```
class Post extends neko.db.Object
{
    public var id : Int;
    public var title : String;
    public var body : String;

    public static var manager = new neko.db.Manager<Post>(Post);
}
```

You also have to create the corresponding table in your SQL database. You can create it and name it "myBlog".

In order to do so, you can use the following SQL statement:

```
CREATE TABLE  'Post' (
'id' INT NOT NULL AUTO_INCREMENT,
'title' TEXT NOT NULL,
'body' LONGTEXT NOT NULL,
PRIMARY KEY ( 'id' )
) ENGINE = MYISAM;
```

Once you have done this, our SQL database is set up correctly and we have objects to work with. You may want to populate it with some dumb posts:

```
INSERT INTO  'expressCafe'.'Post' (
'id' ,
'title' ,
'body'
)
VALUES (
NULL ,  'First Post',  'Hi, this is the first post of this blog!'
), (
NULL ,  'Second post',  'This is the second post in a not so long
series of articles.'
);
```

You may also execute the following if you want two more posts:

```
INSERT INTO  'expressCafe'.'Post' (
'id' ,
'title' ,
'body'
)
VALUES (
NULL , 'Third post',  'This is the third post in our series of
articles.'
), (
NULL , 'Fourth and last post',  'Hi, this is the fourth and last post
of our series!'
);
```

Time for action – Connecting to the database

In our main function, let's initiate the connection to our database and the SPOD system:

```
import Post;

class Main
{
   public static function main()
   {
      //Parameters to connect to the MySQL database
      var cnx = neko.db.Mysql.connect({
            host : "localhost",
            port : 3306,
            database : "myBlog",
            user : "root",
            pass : "",
        });

      //Initialize the SPOD system
        neko.db.Manager.cnx = cnx;
        neko.db.Manager.initialize();


      //We've done our processing, let's clean things and disconnect
        neko.db.Manager.cleanup();
        cnx.close();
   }
}
```

When doing this, we can successfully connect to the database although it won't do anything at the moment.

Now, let's just retrieve our posts from the database by simply adding this:

```
var posts = Post.manager.all();
```

We now have the following:

```
import Post;

class Main
{
    public static function main()
    {
        //Parameters to connect to the MySQL database
        var cnx = neko.db.Mysql.connect({
            host : "localhost",
            port : 3306,
            database : "myBlog",
            user : "root",
            pass : "",
        });

        //Initialize the SPOD system
        neko.db.Manager.cnx = cnx;
        neko.db.Manager.initialize();

        var posts = Post.manager.all();

        //We've done our processing, let's clean things and disconnect
        neko.db.Manager.cleanup();
        cnx.close();
    }
}
```

So, we now have all our Posts at our disposal when we want to use them in our template.

Time for action – Creating our template

Now, let's create a template that will simply take an object with the property `posts` to hold our list of posts.

Add this code to your `template.html` file:

```
<html>
   <head>
      <title>List of Posts</title>
   </head>
   <body>
      <!-- Simply display a greeting -->
      <h1>Hi and welcome on my blog!</h1>
      <!-- Iterate over all Posts -->
      ::foreach posts::
         <!-- Display's the blog post's title -->
         <h2>::title::</h2>
         <!-- Display's the blog post's body -->
         <div>::body::</div>
      ::end::
   </body>
</html>
```

You will also want to include this file as a resource named `template`.

To do so, just add the following to your compilation command:

```
-resource template.html@template
```

That's all it takes.

Time for action – Reading the template from resources

To read our template from resource and store it, we will simply add these lines of code:

```
var templateCode : String;
templateCode = haxe.Resource.getString("template");
```

So, we now have the following:

```
import Post;

class Main
{
   public static function main()
   {
      //Parameters to connect to the MySQL database
      var cnx = neko.db.Mysql.connect({
            host : "localhost",
            port : 3306,
```

```
            database : "myBlog",
            user : "root",
            pass : "",
        });

    //Initialize the SPOD system
        neko.db.Manager.cnx = cnx;
        neko.db.Manager.initialize();

    var posts = Post.manager.all();

    var templateCode : String;
    templateCode = haxe.Resource.getString("template");

    //We've done our processing, let's clean things and disconnect
        neko.db.Manager.cleanup();
        cnx.close();
    }
}
```

Time for action – Executing the template

Now that we have loaded our template's code, we will want to execute it.

In order to do that, we have to take the following steps:

1. Create an instance of `haxe.Template` passing it the value of `templateCode`.

2. Pass an object with a property named `posts` and having our `List of Posts`, as a value so that they can be processed by our template.

3. Execute our template.

4. Print its result.

The first step is done easily with the following line of code:

```
var template = new haxe.Template(templateCode);
```

The second step can be accomplished this way:

```
var context = {posts : posts};
```

Executing the template is just as simple and we don't even need to pass it any macro. We just need to do the following:

```
var result = template.execute(context);
```

Finally, you certainly must have guessed it, to print the result we will just do the usual:

```
neko.Lib.print(result);
```

So, our complete Main class is:

```
import Post;

class Main
{
    public static function main()
    {
        //Parameters to connect to the MySQL database
        var cnx = neko.db.Mysql.connect({
                host : "localhost",
                port : 8889,
                database : "myBlog",
                user : "root",
                pass : "",
              socket : null
            });

        //Initialize the SPOD system
          neko.db.Manager.cnx = cnx;
          neko.db.Manager.initialize();

        var posts = Post.manager.all();

        var templateCode : String;
        templateCode = haxe.Resource.getString("template");

        var template = new haxe.Template(templateCode);

        var context = {posts : posts};

        var result = template.execute(context);

        neko.Lib.print(result);

        //We've done our processing, let's clean things and disconnect
          neko.db.Manager.cleanup();
          cnx.close();
    }
}
```

Time for action – Testing the result

You can simply execute this program and you should get the following output:

```
<html>
    <head>
        <title>List of Posts</title>
    </head>
    <body>
        <!-- Simply display a greeting -->
        <h1>Hi and welcome to my blog!</h1>
        <!-- Iterate over all Posts -->

            <!-- Displays the blog post's title -->
            <h2>First Post</h2>
            <!-- Displays the blog post's body -->
            <div>Hi, this is the first post of this blog!</div>

            <!-- Displays the blog post's title -->
            <h2>Second post</h2>
            <!-- Displays the blog post's body -->
            <div>This is the second post in a not so long series of
            articles.</div>

            <!-- Displays the blog post's title -->
            <h2>Third post</h2>
            <!-- Displays the blog post's body -->
            <div>This is the third post in our series of articles.</div>

            <!-- Displays the blog post's title -->
            <h2>Fourth and last post</h2>
            <!-- Displays the blog post's body -->
            <div>Hi, this is the fourth and last post of our series!
            </div>

    </body>
</html>
```

This is exactly what we were waiting for.

Note that this example is pretty simple but you may want to change the style of posts depending on the author.

In addition, our comments here take up quite a lot of space for the "useful code". Even though our file is pretty small here, it certainly isn't a good idea to almost multiply the size of your file per 2, especially if you're going to make it transit over the Internet. So, you may want to have a look at such things and clean them up.

One last thing: even though in this chapter we've always used our templating system in order to generate HTML, it is also possible to use it to make reference to the haXe templating system to generate any other kind of text-based files. So, you may want to generate XML files using this system. It can be really useful for quite a lot of things.

Pop quiz – Doing the thing

1. Template files can only be loaded from compiled resources?

    a. True

    b. False

2. In templates, you can access the current context object by using:

    a. the __current__ word

    b. the __context__ word

    c. the __now__ word

Have a go hero – Doing more with the thing

Let's imagine we want to take our blog example a bit further: use it as a starting point, and add a link for each blog post in order to delete it.

Summary

In this chapter, we've been talking about the haXe's standard templating system. As we've seen, it's not difficult to use and allows one to do quite a lot of interesting things such as easily generating an HTML page or generating other kind of text-files such as XML files (and even any kind of interface that uses XML as a describing language).

Specifically, we covered how to instantiate templates and give a context to them. We've also learnt how to do testing and branching in templates and calling code from them.

This chapter, although quite simple, exposes important information that you will certainly use many times while developing applications.

Also, remember that you cannot access an object's property using a template. This is a very important limitation of haxe.Template.

Now that we've learned about templates we're ready to learn about how to interface haXe with the platform you're targeting.

10
Interfacing with the Target Platform

Working with your platform.

Being able to use the interns of the platform you are targeting or to work with native code can be really useful: it may lead to being able to easily use some functionality of a library or to optimize your code. However, it also has its drawbacks.

We have now learned about the basics of haXe and are going to get into more technical stuff—interfacing with the target platform. Doing so may be really useful for several things, such as using a library that has been written for the target platform. It is sometimes useful in order to optimize your code too.

In this chapter we will:

◆ Learn about what extern classes are
◆ The magic functions
◆ Interfacing with native code

So, if you are ready, let's go on!

Extern classes

Extern classes allow one to tell the compiler what classes exist outside of your own code. This way, the compiler won't tell you that the class does not exist and it will also know what fields exist in it and what their type is.

Time for action – Writing an extern

Imagine that we are writing a `User` class in JavaScript:

```
function User()
{
    var name;
    var age;
}
User.prototype.outputInfo = function()
{
    var el = document.createElement("div");
    el.innerHTML = this.name+"("+ this.age+")";
    document.body.appendChild(el);
}
```

Now, if we want to use this class from our haXe application, then we have to write the corresponding `extern` class as follows:

```
extern class User
{
    public var name:String;
    public var age:Int;
    public function outputInfo():Void;
    public function new():Void;
}
```

There are several things that you should note:

- You have to prefix your class declaration with the `extern` keyword
- We do not write any code inside function declaration
- Constructors should be declared returning `Void`

What just happened?

We have written an extern class, explaining to the compiler that the `User` class exists outside our code and can be used from it.

Using an extern

Now, we can use this class in our haXe code:

```
class Main
{
    public static function main()
```

```
    {
        var u1 = new User();
        u1.name = "Benjamin";
        u1.age = 22;
        var u2 = new User();
        u2.name = "Bear";
        u2.age = 54;
        u1.outputInfo();
        u2.outputInfo();
    }
}
```

Then you can create the following HTML page:

```
<!DOCTYPE html PUBLIC "-//W3C//DTD XHTML 1.0 Transitional//EN"
    "http://www.w3.org/TR/xhtml1/DTD/xhtml1-transitional.dtd">
<html xmlns="http://www.w3.org/1999/xhtml" xml:lang="en" lang="en">
<head>
    <meta http-equiv="Content-Type" content="text/html;
        charset=utf-8"/>

    <title>Extern Example</title>
    <script type="text/javascript">
        function User()
        {
            var name;
            var age;
        }
        User.prototype.outputInfo = function()
        {
            var el = document.createElement("div");
            el.innerHTML = this.name + " ( " + this.age + " )";
            document.body.appendChild(el);
        }
    </script>
</head>

<body>

<script type="text/javascript" src="TestUser.js">
</script>
</body>
</html>
```

You can compile this sample with the following command:

```
haxe -js TestUser.js -main Main
```

This will output the following in our browser:

Benjamin (22)

Bear (54)

This is exactly what we could expect when looking at the JS code.

Class path

Note that the compiler expects the native class to have the same path as the extern class you are creating.

This can be a problem as you may wish to have something more meaningful than the native class path. Also, and more importantly, it can be a real stopper because of some incompatibilities; for example, a few languages may allow class names that begin with lowercase letters while haXe doesn't.

There is a solution to circumvent this problem and this comes as the @:native metadata. This metadata will take a string as a parameter. The compiler will then know that the path to the native class is indeed the one provided as a string. However, this does not change anything to the path you are going to use in your haXe code.

Let's see a simple example:

```
class ExExtern
{

    public function new()
    {

    }

    public static function main():Void
    {
        MyExtern.test();
    }
}

@:native("my.extern.Path") extern class MyExtern
{
    public static function test():Void;
}
```

This code will fail at runtime if we do not have a class named `my.extern.Path`. However, let's generate the JS code for it and have a look at the generated file. At the beginning of it, you will see the following:

```
ExExtern.main = function() {
    my.extern.Path.test();
}
```

That shows that the compiler has automatically replaced the path `MyExtern` with the `my.extern.Path` one.

Limitations

Note that extern classes won't support subclassing on some targets and at the time of writing this book, they do not work at all on the C++ target.

The __init__ magic

There is a special magic function named `__init__` that is executed when a class is initialized. Each class can have this function.

This function is the only one that can contain code in an extern class.

It can be particularly useful when working with extern classes; for example, imagine you have a class named `Post` written in pure PHP and you want to use it from your haXe code. This class is in the `classes/post.php` file. We want to be able to use it from haXe code as a class named `mySystem.Post`.

The first thing we will have to do is to tell the PHP runtime to load the `classes/post.php` file before using the `mySystem.Post` class. We can do so by using the `__init__` function as follows:

```
package mySystem;

@:native("post") extern class Post
{
    public var name:String;
    public var body:String;
    public function new():Void;

    public static function __init__()
    {
        untyped __call__("require_once", "classes/post.php");
    }
}
```

By doing it this way, we will know that the `__init__` function of the `mySystem.Post` class will be called before our first use of the `Post` class.

The line beginning with `untyped` makes use of the magic `__call__` function. We will see later how this function works in more detail. All we need to know at the moment is that it allows us, when targeting PHP, to call the function named as what is passed as first argument, with passing it arguments that are following. So here, it is as if we had written the following in PHP:

```
require_once("classes/posts.php");
```

This way, we know that the file that does really contain the PHP code for the class will be loaded when it is needed.

Native types and haXe types

haXe defines some types that may already exist in the target platform.

For example, haXe defines the `Array` class. The `Array` class is already defined on almost all target platforms. The thing is that on some targets, the haXe array and the native array may indeed be different.

In such cases, when working with externs, you may need to convert from a haXe array to a native array and vice-versa.

You have to pay particular attention to that when working with Neko and PHP.

The Neko and PHP cases

If you are targeting Neko or PHP, then you will have to pay particular attention to array and string. Indeed, in the Neko and PHP packages, you will find the native array and native string types.

There are also 'functions and methods that you can use to convert a native type to the haXe one.

PHP functions

The following are the functions that you can use in PHP to convert from native types to haXe types:

Functions	Explanation
php.Lib.associativeArrayOfHash	This function creates a native PHP array from a haXe hash. Elements contained inside the hash are not converted from the haXe type to the native types even if needed.
php.Lib.hashOfAssociativeArray	This function creates a haXe hash from a PHP array. Elements contained inside the array are not automatically converted.
php.Lib.toHaxeArray	This function takes a native array and returns a haXe array. Elements contained inside the native array are not automatically converted.
php.Lib.toNativeArray	This function takes a haXe array and returns a native array. Elements contained inside the haXe array are not automatically converted.

You should remember the following two things:

1. Elements contained inside containers (such as arrays and hash hashes) are not automatically converted, even if they need to be. You have to do it on your own.

2. When converting from a PHP native array to a haXe array, if the PHP array's indexes are not indexes following each other, the conversion will fail. You can work around that by using the PHP array_values function that re-indexes an array.

Neko functions

When targeting Neko, you only have two functions to use:

Function	Explanation
neko.Lib.haxeToNeko	This function converts a haXe value to the corresponding Neko native value. Elements inside containers are not automatically converted.
neko.Lib.nekoToHaxe	This function converts a Neko value to the corresponding haXe value. Elements inside containers are not automatically converted.

Once again, you have to remember the fact that elements inside containers are not automatically converted and you may need to do it manually.

Magic functions

Magic functions are special functions that should be handled with care—they are very useful to interface with your target platform, but they can produce undefined behavior if they are not correctly used. In addition, they do not provide any kind of typing as they can only be used inside an untyped block.

Available magic functions are different from one platform to another and therefore, if you are targeting several platforms, you really have to be careful and should consider using conditional compilation.

The Flash magic

The Flash platform is certainly the one with the most magic functions. Certainly, you will not use all of them straight away, but they can always be useful. So, let's go on with them.

In addition, some of them are only available when targeting a specific version of Flash.

__new__

Available in Flash 6 to 10

The `__new__` magic function allows you to create an instance of a class. Its syntax is as follows:

```
__new__(cl : Dynamic, param1 : Dynamic, param2 : Dynamic,…);
```

As you can see, it is very convenient since you can pass as many arguments as needed by the constructor of your class.

__arguments__

Available in Flash 6 to 10

The `__arguments__` magic function allows you to access Flash's arguments' special variable. It is a variable containing all of the arguments that were passed to the function. The syntax is as follows:

```
__arguments__
```

__typeof__

Available in Flash 6 to 10

This magic function has the following syntax:

```
__typeof__(o)
```

It is similar to calling `typeof` in ActionScript.

It also has the following syntax:

```
__typeof__(o,cl)
```

This is similar to writing as `o` instanceof `cl` in ActionScript.

__delete__

Available in Flash 6 to 10

The `__delete__` magic function has the following syntax:

```
__delete__(obj, field)
```

It does exactly the same thing as `delete` does in ActionScript.

__eval__

Available in Flash 6 to 7

The `__eval__` function has the following syntax:

```
__eval__(e)
```

It evaluates the expression that is given to it.

__gettimer__

Available in Flash 6 to 10

The __gettimer__ magic function has the following syntax:

```
__gettimer__()
```

It does exactly the same thing as gettimer in ActionScript.

__geturl__

Available in Flash 6 to 10

The __geturl__ magic function has the following syntax:

```
__geturl__(e1, e1)
```

It does the same thing as in ActionScript.

__instanceof__

Available in Flash 6 to 10

The __instanceof__ magic function has the following syntax:

```
__instanceof__(o, cl)
```

This is similar to writing o instanceof cl in ActionScript.

__random__

 Available in Flash 6 to 8

The __random__ magic function has the following syntax:

    __random__(e1)

It does the same thing as in ActionScript.

__trace__

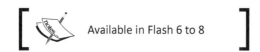 Available in Flash 6 to 8

The __trace__ magic function has the following syntax:

    __trace__(e)

It allows one to access the native trace function of ActionScript.

__keys__

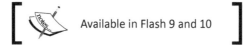 Available in Flash 9 and 10

This magic function has the following syntax:

    __keys__(o)

It returns an array containing all properties that can be enumerated in o.

__global__

Available in Flash 9 and 10

The __global__ magic is not a function but an array that can be accessed using strings as indexes. It gives you access to the top-level package that exists in ActionScript. Here is an example of how to use it to retrieve the string type:

```
untyped __global__["String"];
```

__as__

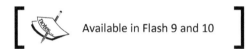

Available in Flash 9 and 10

The __as__ magic function has the following syntax:

```
__as__(e, t)
```

It does the same thing as in ActionScript.

__is__

Available in Flash 9 and 10

This magic function has the following syntax:

```
__is__(e, t)
```

It does the same thing as in ActionScript.

__in__

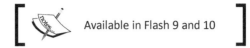

Available in Flash 9 and 10

This function has the following syntax:

```
__in__(e, f)
```

It does the same thing as in ActionScript.

The Neko magic

Native functions in Neko are called `builtins` and in order to call them from haXe, you can use the `__dollar__` word to replace the $ sign that is normally used at the beginning of `builtins`.

It is that simple.

Arrays and strings

When targeting Neko, haXe arrays and haXe strings are wrappers. This means that they store the native array and string inside a field and use this object in order to give you the functions of haXe array.

- The native array is stored inside the `__a` field of a haXe array.
- The native string is stored inside the `__s` field of a haXe string.

However, in order to be sure that you won't have problems later, in the way that haXe arrays and strings work in regard to the native ones, you should use `neko.Lib.haxeToNeko`.

The PHP magic

The PHP target has the following four magic functions:

__php__

The `__php__` magic function allows you to directly print some PHP code inside the output generated by the compiler. For example:

```
untyped __php__("echo('Hello World');");
```

__call__

This magic function has the following syntax:

```
__call__(func : String, p1, p2, p3, p4…);
```

It allows you to call a function with as many parameters as you want. It allows returns that the function returns.

__var__

This magic function allows you to retrieve values from global variables such as $_SERVER. Its syntax is as follows:

```
__var__(globalName : String, ?valueToAccess : String);
```

__physeq__

This magic function allows checking for physical equality between two expressions. Its syntax is the following:

```
__physeq__(e1, e2)
```

Have a go hero – Wrapping parameters in an array

Imagine that you are writing a Flash application. In this application, you have to create a function that takes a variable number of parameters and returns a newly created array with all of these parameters in the reverse order.

Pop quiz – Doing the things

1. It is possible to define the native path to an extern class by using:

   a. The @:native metadata

   b. The @:realpath metadata

   c. It is not possible

2. PHP magic functions can be accessed when targeting Neko:

   a. True

   b. False

3. The __init__ function can contain code even in extern class:

   a. True

   b. False

Summary

In this chapter, we've learned how you can interface your haXe code with your target platform by using magic functions and using the __init__ magic. We have also seen how to use several magic functions.

Now that we've seen how to interface haXe code with the target platform, we are going to create a completely dynamic website with haXe targeting Javascript.

11
A Dynamic Website Using JavaScript

Extensive use of JavaScript.

If you create a website using haXe, then you will certainly want to use some JavaScript in it. To do this requires some experience and can be achieved if you pay attention to some things.

We have learned many things about haXe. Well enough for you to use it daily and use it with ease day after day. In this chapter, we will put some things into practice and learn about how one can create a website using haXe/Javascript.

In this chapter, we will:

- See what kind of caveats one has to avoid
- Manipulate the DOM
- Interface with the browser

After that, we will have an exercise.

Manipulating the DOM

While we will be able to use haXe to target JavaScript and create a website, haXe doesn't really provide us with any abstraction layers over the DOM.

We will try to remember some things about the DOM and see how it is exposed by haXe.

The browser's DOM

The browser's **DOM** (**Document Object Model**) defines what objects the browser should expose to our application in order to represent the document (the HTML page) and to provide us with some functionality (think about the date object).

It is in the DOM that the type of each HTML object (such as a list, an item in a list, a header, and so on) is defined. In addition, in the DOM it is defined that, for example, an HTML node should have an `appendChild` function in order to allow the addition of child nodes.

Let's remember some basics of the DOM manipulation in JavaScript.

Nodes

Everything in HTML is a node. There are several types of nodes, we won't list them all here, but what we need to remember is that there are two big ones when manipulating the DOM, which are as follows:

- The ones that have a markup around them (pre, p, span, div, and so on)
- Text nodes

So, texts are also nodes, even if we don't have markup around them. So when you have the following markup:

```
<p>Hello World</p>
```

You indeed have a node "p" (it is an element) and inside it, there is a text-node.

Now, how can we construct the equivalent to this markup in JavaScript?

The DOM provides the following two methods inside the document object that are useful:

- `createElement`
- `createTextNode`

The first one allows you to create an element. You just have to pass the name of the markup as a parameter. The second one allows you to create text nodes. You can pass it the text of the node to be created as a parameter.

Ok, so in JavaScript, we would do the following:

```
var pEl = document.createElement("p");
var text = document.createTextNode("Hello World");
pEl.appendChild(text);

//And we can add it to the document by doing:
document.body.appendChild(pEl);
```

In haXe, we will basically do the same thing as haXe simply offers us access to the HTML DOM.

Note however that there is nothing except types in the global scope in haXe. Therefore, document is not available through the global scope as it is in JavaScript.

So, you may wonder how we are going to manage accessing it.

Well, it is pretty simple; the `js.Lib` class holds a reference to document, so we can do that:

```
class Main
{
    public static function main(): Void
    {
        var pEl = js.Lib.document.createElement("p");
        var text = js.Lib.document.createTextNode("Hello World");
        pEl.appendChild(text);

        //Add it to the body of the document:
        js.Lib.document.body.appendChild(pEl);
    }
}
```

Therefore, at first you may wonder why we would want to do it in haXe since it seems to be much longer and complicated.

Well, the advantages in such a simple case are quite limited. However, in more complex programs, having a compiler to tell you when you're using an undefined variable is really valuable and can help you refactor the code and avoid very long debugging phases for a small error in the name of a variable or because you mixed some types.

Nevertheless, remember the `import` keyword? Well, we can use it in order to reduce the amount of typing required:

```
import js.Lib;

class Main
{
    public static function main(): Void
    {
        var pEl = Lib.document.createElement("p");
        var text = Lib.document.createTextNode("Hello World");
        pEl.appendChild(text);

        //Add it to the body of the document:
        Lib.document.body.appendChild(pEl);
    }
}
```

In addition, nothing prevents us from storing a reference to document in order to shorten things even more:

```
import js.Lib;

class Main
{
    public static function main(): Void
    {
        var document = Lib.document;
        var pEl = document.createElement("p");
        var text =document.createTextNode("Hello World");
        pEl.appendChild(text);

        //Add it to the body of the document:
        document.body.appendChild(pEl);
    }
}
```

Events

Events are one of the most important things when developing an application in JavaScript, mostly because it is through events that the user interacts with your application.

So, for example, an event is raised when the user clicks on a button.

Unfortunately, even though events are one of the most important pieces of the DOM, the specifications for events are one of the least respected across implementations of the DOM in browsers.

Level 1

In level 1, one can handle events by simply setting fields of an object to a function. For example, in JavaScript:

```
var but = document.createElement("button");
but.onclick = function (event) { alert('You clicked.'); };
```

In this example, we create a button and define the function that will be executed when it is clicked by giving it a reference to an anonymous function.

You can also use a named function. What is pretty interesting with event handlers in JavaScript is their scope—if you use the this keyword, it will reference the button.

This is quite awkward and not what we expect in haXe. Let's hope that in haXe, the compiler automatically makes sure that the this keyword will point to the good scope (in other words: it makes sure this points to the current object).

So, in haXe we can do the following:

```
import js.Lib;
import js.Dom;

class Main
{
    private var id : String;

    public function new()
    {

    }

    public function clickHandler(ev : js.Event)
    {
        js.Lib.alert("You clicked. Click handled by" + this.id);
    }

    public static function main(): Void
    {
        var nMain = new Main();
        nMain.id = "abc";

        var document = Lib.document;
        var pEl = document.createElement("button");
        var text =document.createTextNode("Hello World");
        pEl.appendChild(text);
        pEl.onclick = nMain.clickHandler;

        //Add it to the body of the document:
        document.body.appendChild(pEl);
    }
}
```

Moreover, you will see the abc ID appearing while clicking, proving that the this keyword has the scope we were expecting.

Also, note that haXe offers an event type. The only problem with this type is that some browsers actually do have a different signature for it.

That is why we discussed earlier that haXe doesn't provide any kind of abstraction on top of JavaScript for DOM manipulation.

Level 2

In level 2, one uses listeners.

The basic thing is to register one or several functions to be called when a specific event happens. This is a very convenient way of handling events; unfortunately, Internet Explorer up to Version 8 (included) does not support the same interface as other browsers.

Let's see how other browsers handle it.

We can use the `addEventListener` function that can take three parameters:

◆ The type of event to be handled (as a string)

◆ The listener (a function)

◆ A Boolean saying if we want to handle the event in the capture phase or in the bubbling phase

Note that the target is the element in which the event took place.

In the capture phase, the event goes from the outermost element containing the target to the innermost one. Then the event fires in the target and then comes the bubbling phase in which the event goes from the innermost element to the outermost one. Note that some events do not go through the bubbling phase.

The haXe API doesn't provide access to the `addEventListener` function, but it is possible to use it in an untyped block or by declaring the variable as `Dynamic`.

Also, note that Internet Explorer uses an `attachEvent` method which is quite similar to `addEventListener`.

Time for action – Using events from the DOM level 0

We are going to write a small example of using events from the DOM level 0.

In this example, we will have a table listing a user's first and last name. We will also have a simple form to add a user to the list. Everything will be managed only by JavaScript.

So, at first, let's create our HTML file with the markup for the table presenting our list of users and for our little form too.

We will also load our haXe generated JavaScript file:

```
<!DOCTYPE html PUBLIC "-//W3C//DTD XHTML 1.0 Transitional//EN"
    "http://www.w3.org/TR/xhtml1/DTD/xhtml1-transitional.dtd">

<html xmlns="http://www.w3.org/1999/xhtml" xml:lang="en" lang="en">
```

```
<head>
    <meta http-equiv="Content-Type" content="text/html;
      charset=utf-8"/>

    <title>User List</title>

</head>

<body>
<!-- Create the table for the list -->
<table id="userList">
<tr id="formRow">
    <td><input type="text" id="formFirstName"/></td>
    <td><input type="text" id="formLastName"/></td>
    <td><button id="formConfirm">Add</button></td>
</tr>
</table>


<!-- Load our haXe generated Javascript code -->
<script type="text/javascript" src="Main.js">
</script>
</body>
</html>
```

Now, let's move on to the haXe code:

```
import js.Lib;
import js.Dom;

class Main
{
    private static var formFirstName:js.Text;
    private static var formLastName:js.Text;
    private static var formConfirm:js.Button;
    private static var userListBody:js.HtmlDom;

    public static function main():Void
    {
        //Get reference to our three elements in the form
        formFirstName = cast Lib.document.getElementById("formFirstName");
        formLastName = cast Lib.document.getElementById("formLastName");
        formConfirm = cast Lib.document.getElementById("formConfirm");
        //And to the table body
```

```
        userListBody = untyped Lib.document.getElementById
          ("userList").tBodies[0];

        //Set the event handler when clicking on button
        formConfirm.onclick = confirm;
    }

    public static function confirm(ev:js.Event)
    {
        //Control that both fields are filled
        if(formFirstName.value == "" || formLastName.value == "")
            return;
        addUser(formFirstName.value, formLastName.value);
    }

    public static function addUser(firstName:String, lastName: String)
    {
        //Create a new row
        var row = Lib.document.createElement("tr");
        //Create a new cell for first name
        var firstNameCell = Lib.document.createElement("td");
        //Fill it
        firstNameCell.appendChild(Lib.document.createTextNode(firstName));
        //Add it to the row
        row.appendChild(firstNameCell);

        //Create a new cell for last name
        var lastNameCell = Lib.document.createElement("td");
        //Fill it
        firstNameCell.appendChild(Lib.document.createTextNode(lastName));
        //Add it to the row
        row.appendChild(lastNameCell);

        //Insert the new row before the "form row"
        userListBody.insertBefore(row, formConfirm.parentNode.parentNode);

        //Clean fields
        formFirstName.value = "";
        formLastName.value = "";
    }
}
```

What just happened?

If you try it, you should see that it works just as expected.

In the HTML code, we have defined the different elements for our UI and assigned them some IDs. We also load the JS program that will be generated from our haXe code.

Then, in the main function, we get references to the UI elements from the HTML markup and add the `onclick` handler on the button. Once this is done and when the user clicks on the button, the `confirm` function will be called.

Time for action – Using DOM level 2 events

In level 2, there is a function named `removeEventListener` (`detachEvent` is the equivalent of it in Internet Explorer's model).

This function allows one to remove an event listener. It only needs the type of the event (as a string) and the listener to be removed.

Unfortunately, every time you pass a reference to a function, the haXe compiler creates a closure. Closures are like functions enclosing functions and as such, the reference you pass to `addEventListener` and the one you pass to `removeEventListener` will never be equal, resulting in the `removeEventListener` function not being able to remove the listener.

This can be tested in a very simple way.

Create an HTML file with the markup for two buttons and load our code as follows:

```
<!DOCTYPE html PUBLIC "-//W3C//DTD XHTML 1.0 Transitional//EN"
    "http://www.w3.org/TR/xhtml1/DTD/xhtml1-transitional.dtd">

<html xmlns="http://www.w3.org/1999/xhtml" xml:lang="en" lang="en">
<head>
    <meta http-equiv="Content-Type" content="text/html;
      charset=utf-8"/>

    <title>User List</title>

</head>

<body>

<button id='button1'>Click here</button>
<button id='button2'>Remove handler</button>
```

```
<!-- Load our haXe generated Javascript code -->
<script type="text/javascript" src="Main.js">
</script>
</body>
</html>
```

Then, create the following haXe code:

```
import js.Lib;
import js.Dom;

class Main
{
    static var but1:js.Button;
    static var but2:js.Button;

    public static function main():Void
    {
        but1 = cast Lib.document.getElementById("button1");
        but2 = cast Lib.document.getElementById("button2");

        untyped but1.addEventListener("click", clickHandler);
        but2.onclick = removeHandler;
    }

    public static function clickHandler(ev:js.Event)
    {
        js.Lib.alert("You've clicked.");
    }

    public static function removeHandler(ev:js.Event)
    {
        untyped but1.removeEventListener("click", clickHandler);
    }
}
```

What just happened?

We have simply created a HTML page with two buttons—the first one has an event handler set with addEventHandler while the second one has an event handler used to remove the first one.

Now, if you load the page and click the first button, you will see an alert. Click on the second button; that should remove the listener on the first button, and finally, click on the first one again. As you can see, the alert still appears although it should not.

Time for action – Working around by storing reference to functions

You can work around this problem by storing references to functions:

```
import js.Lib;
import js.Dom;

class Main
{
    static var but1:js.Button;
    static var but2:js.Button;
    static var myHandler:js.Event->Void;

    public static function main(): Void
    {
        but1 = cast Lib.document.getElementById("button1");
        but2 = cast Lib.document.getElementById("button2");

        myHandler = clickHandler;

        untyped but1.addEventListener("click", myHandler);
        but2.onclick = removeHandler;
    }

    public static function clickHandler(ev : js.Event)
    {
        js.Lib.alert("You've clcked.");
    }

    public static function removeHandler(ev:js.Event)
    {
        untyped but1.removeEventListener("click", myHandler);
    }
}
```

What just happened?

Note the use of the myHandler variable—now, instead of creating a new closure every time, we store one into myHandler. This way, it is possible to remove our function handler.

Note that this problem regarding function reference doesn't only occur when manipulating removeEventListener, it can occur with any method that has to compare two functions.

Have a go hero – A dynamic website with JavaScript

Now that we've learned how to target JavaScript with haXe and how to interact with the DOM, we should try to create some dynamic website.

We will create a front-end that will get a list of computers from an XML file.

We will present our list of computers in a table and should be able to add some to it. We should also be able to delete them.

Note that adding and deleting won't change the XML file as that would be beyond the scope of this chapter and we have already seen how to work with files.

In addition, we will try to use a MVC design. So, we will have a computer model; a view that will be our main and only HTML file to display the list of computers and a class to control this view.

Time for action – Setting up the model

First, let's create our computer model.

We need to have the following data about the computers:

◆   Their names
◆   The operating systems they are running

Note that the OS field will use an enum with the three mainly used OS fields and an "Other" field.

Therefore, let's create our `Computer.hx` file with the following code in the `computerList.models` namespace:

```
package computerList.models;

class Computer
{
   public var name:String;
   public var operatingSystem : OS;

   public function new()
   {

   }
}

enum OS
{
```

```
    Windows;
    Linux(distro:String);
    MacOSX;
    Other(name:String);
}
```

That is all we to write in our model at the moment.

Time for action – Setting up our view

Now, let's set up our view.

As we discussed earlier, we will create it as an HTML file. We will need to define the markup to display our computers and also to add one.

Basically, we will have:

- A table to list the computers
- A "name" text-field to create a computer
- An "OS" combobox
- A "details" text-field is the OS chosen allows for more details to be given
- An "Add" button

This file will also integrate our JavaScript generated file.

So, let's create our `ComputerList.html` file as follows:

```
<!DOCTYPE html PUBLIC "-//W3C//DTD XHTML 1.0 Transitional//EN"
    "http://www.w3.org/TR/xhtml1/DTD/xhtml1-transitional.dtd">

<html xmlns="http://www.w3.org/1999/xhtml" xml:lang="en" lang="en">
<head>
    <meta http-equiv="Content-Type" content="text/html;
      charset=utf-8"/>

    <title>ComputerList</title>

</head>

<body>
    <!-- Our table listing computers -->
    <table id='listTable'>
      <!-- List headers -->
      <thead>
```

```
        <tr>
            <td>Computer</td>
            <td>Operating System</td>
            <td colspan="2">Details</td>
        </tr>
    </thead>
    <!-- Create the body in which our data will appear -->
    <tbody>
    </tbody>
    <!-- The 'form' to add a computer -->
    <tfoot>
        <tr>
            <td>
                <input type='text' id='name'>
            </td>
            <td>
                <!-- The selectbox to choose OS -->
                <select id='OS'>
                    <option value='macosx'>MacOSX</option>
                    <option value='windows'>Windows</option>
                    <option value='linux'>Linux</option>
                </select>
            </td>
            <td>
                <input type='text' id='details'>
            </td>
            <td>
                <button id='add'>Add</button>
            </td>
        </tr>
    </tfoot>
    </table>

    <!-- Include our script -->
    <script src="ComputerList.js" type="text/javascript">
    </script>
</body>
</html>
```

What just happened?

In this code, we created the form to be displayed and included the JS file that is going to be created from our haXe code.

Now, let's move on to our controller!

Time for action – Setting up the controller

We will set up our controller as `computerList.controllers.`
`ComputerListController`.

It will have to handle actions on the different view's elements (particularly when the user clicks the add button).

Note that we will create another view after that for each row of the table (it will be a `ComputerView`).

Therefore, here is our `ComputerListController.hx` file:

```
package computerList.controllers;

import js.Dom;
import js.Lib;
import computerList.models.Computer;

class ComputerListController
{
    var listBody:js.HtmlDom;
    var nameField:js.Text;
    var osField:js.Select;
    var detailsField:js.Text;
    var addButton:js.Button;

    public function new()
    {
        listBody = untyped Lib.document.getElementById
            ("listTable").tBodies[0];
        nameField = cast Lib.document.getElementById("name");
        osField = cast Lib.document.getElementById("OS");
        detailsField = cast Lib.document.getElementById("details");
        addButton = cast Lib.document.getElementById("add");

        //Add Listener
        addButton.onclick = handleAdd;
    }

    public function handleAdd(ev : js.Event)
    {
        addComputer(nameField.value, osField.value, detailsField.value);
    }
```

```
public function addComputer(name:String, os:String, details:String)
{
    var nComp = new Computer();
    nComp.name = name;
    nComp.operatingSystem = switch(os)
                    {
                        case "linux":
                            OS.Linux(details);
                        case "macosx":
                            OS.MacOSX;
                        case "windows":
                            OS.Windows;
                        case "other":
                            OS.Other(details);
                    };

    //Create the Computer's view and add its main HTML node to
    the table
    var view = new computerList.views.ComputerView(nComp);
    view.onDelete = onComputerDelete;
    listBody.appendChild(view.mainNode);

    //Add it to our global list
    ComputerList.computers.add(nComp);

    //Clear fields
    nameField.value = "";
    osField.value = null;
    detailsField.value = "";
}

public function onComputerDelete(computerView:
    computerList.views.ComputerView)
{
    listBody.removeChild(computerView.mainNode);
}
}
```

Time for action – Creating a computer view

Now, let's create a simple view for `Computer`. It will be named `computerList.views.`
`ComputerView`:

```
package computerList.views;

import computerList.models.Computer;
import js.Dom;
import js.Lib;

class ComputerView
{
    var computer:Computer;
    public var mainNode:js.HtmlDom;

    //To let the parent view know when we delete our object
    public var on Delete:ComputerView -> Void;

    public function new(comp:Computer)
    {
        computer = comp;
        mainNode = Lib.document.createElement("tr");
        var nameCell = Lib.document.createElement("td");
        nameCell.appendChild(Lib.document.createTextNode(computer.name));
        var osCell = Lib.document.createElement("td");
        var detailsCell = Lib.document.createElement("td");
        osCell.appendChild(Lib.document.createTextNode)
                switch(computer.operatingSystem)
                {
                    case Linux(distro):
                        detailsCell.appendChild(Lib.document.
                        createTextNode(distro));
                        "Linux";
                    case MacOSX:
                        "MacOSX";
                    case Windows:
                        "Windows";
                    case Other(name):
                        detailsCell.appendChild(Lib.document.
                        createTextNode(name));
                        "Other";
                }
            ));

        var deleteCell = Lib.document.createElement("td");
        var deleteButton = Lib.document.createElement("button");
        deleteButton.appendChild(Lib.document.createTextNode("Del"));
        deleteCell.appendChild(deleteButton);
```

```
        mainNode.appendChild(nameCell);
        mainNode.appendChild(osCell);
        mainNode.appendChild(detailsCell);
        mainNode.appendChild(deleteCell);

        deleteButton.onclick = delete;
    }

    public function delete(ev:js.Event)
    {
        //Remove from global list
        ComputerList.computers.remove(this.computer);
        //Let the parent view know
        this.onDelete(this);
    }
}
```

What just happened?

When a new instance of this class is created, it creates DOM elements needed to represent the instance of the Computer class that is passed to it.

As you can see, this view makes everything programmatical and is indeed also a controller. This is quite acceptable in our case for the sake of simplicity and because it doesn't do anything too complicated.

The main class

Here is our main class; it contains the global list of computers:

```
import computerList.models.Computer;

class ComputerList
{
    public static var computers = new List<Computer>();

    public static function main():Void
    {
        new computerList.controllers.ComputerListController();
    }
}
```

Now, you can test our application and see that it works!

Summary

In this chapter, we have seen how to target JavaScript with haXe in order to manipulate the DOM.

Specifically, we covered:

- How the haXe API lets us manipulate the DOM
- What kind of caveats to avoid
- How we can handle events with haXe

Now, for our last chapter, we are going to write a game in Flash!

12

Creating a Game with haXe and Flash

Assets imports and event handling.

In order to create a game, there are two very important things that you will need to do. The first one is to import images and sounds inside your SWF and to use them in your haXe code. The second one is to handle events, such as keyboard strokes.

This is our last chapter! We now know enough about haXe to create a Flash game with it. In this chapter, we will learn about assets embedding and usage, and events handling. We will learn to do that by targeting Flash 9 and more.

In this chapter, we will:

◆ Learn how to embed assets

◆ Learn how to use embedded assets

◆ Learn how to handle events

Moreover, at the end of this chapter, we will create a small game making use of this.

Embedding assets

Before we can use images or sounds in our applications for Flash, we should embed these assets. The haXe compiler does not directly manage that, but there are several tools that can be used to do it, such as the following:

◆ SWFMILL

◆ SamHaXe-Open

- ◆ The Flash IDE
- ◆ Some other tools that can export to SWF format

SWFMILL has been around for years, even before haXe. So, in this chapter, we are going to see how to use it.

Time for action – Installing SWFMILL

Go to the SWFMILL website at `www.swfmill.org` and download the binary for your operating system.

If you are using a Linux distribution, then you may also want to have a look in its repository as it may contain some binaries for SWFMILL.

Time for action – Creating a library

We will use SWFMILL to create a SWF file containing all our assets.

After that, we will instruct the haXe compiler to embed this SWF file in the one it is going to produce.

Creating a library can be made quite easily with SWFMILL using a XML language to describe it. Let's have a look at an XML file that will allow us to embed one image as a clip:

```xml
<?xml version="1.0" encoding="utf-8"?>
<movie width="60" height="20" framerate="20"
  frames="1" as3="1" version="9">
<frame>
<library>
   <clip id="Ship" import="image/ship.jpg"/>
</library>
</frame>
</movie>
```

Note that this clip will have the linkage ID as `Ship` and is the image located at `image/ship.jpg` (this is relative to the current working directory when we will run SWFMILL).

Note that one can also have bitmap tags and sound tags (there are also others available, but we won't use them).

After having created this file, you can open a terminal and execute SWFMILL as follows:

`swfmill simple assets.xml assets.swf`

This will take the definition from `assets.xml` and generate the `assets.swf` file containing every asset you have defined.

Time for action – Using assets

To use an asset, we will have to create a class with the same name as its linkage ID. Depending on the tag we have used, this class should be of a different type as shown in the following table:

Tag	haXe Type
clip	flash.display.MovieClip
sound	flash.display.MovieClip
bitmap	flash.display.Bitmap

Therefore, for example, for our Ship we should create the following class:

```
import flash.display.MovieClip;

@:bind class Ship extends MovieClip
{
    public function new()
    {
        super();
    }
}
```

We can then add an instance of it on our main timeline:

```
@:bind class TestAssets
{
    public static function main(): Void
    {
        var ship = new Ship();
        flash.Lib.current.stage.addChild(ship);
    }
}
```

We will compile and run this as usual, but we need to add an option to our compilation instructions. This option is the -swf-lib that will instruct the compiler to embed our SWF containing our assets:

```
-swf-lib assets.swf
```

It is that simple. Then, compile as usual and run your SWF. You should see your asset on the stage.

Event handling

Event handling in AS3 is pretty simple; it basically works by registering listeners to an event.

To do so, we will call the `addEventListener` function on the object we want to listen to the event on. We will have to pass the name of the event we want to listen to (this is done by passing a `String`, these strings are stored as statics inside classes in the `flash.events` package) and a function to handle the event.

The following is an example:

```
public static function main(): Void
{
    flash.Lib.current.stage.addEventListener
      (flash.events.KeyboardEvent.KEY_DOWN, keyDown);
}
private static function keyDown(args : flash.events.KeyboardEvent)
{
    trace(args.keyCode);
    switch(args.keyCode)
    {
        case flash.ui.Keyboard.LEFT: //Left
            trace("Left");
            horizontalSpeed = -10;
        case flash.ui.Keyboard.RIGHT: //Right
            trace("Right");
            horizontalSpeed = 10;
    }
}
```

In this example, the `keyDown` function will be called every time a key is pressed.

The haXe compiler will expect you to provide a listener of type `Dynamic->Void`, but it is possible to give a more precise type to the parameter your listener will expect.

For example, if you took your string describing your event from `flash.events.KeyboardEvent`, you could expect the parameter to be of type `flash.events.KeyboardEvent`.

Have a go hero – A game with Flash

As promised in the beginning of this chapter, we are going to write a simple game with haXe targeting Flash.

The first thing we have to do is to find our "game design".

The game design

We will create a very basic game. Our scene will be 400x400 pixels. The player will control a 50px per 100px guy at the bottom of the screen and will be able to move it on the horizontal axis by using his keyboard.

Balls (red or black) will appear randomly at a fixed interval of time at the top of the screen and at a random position on the horizontal axis. They will then fall across the screen.

The player should get the red ones, but avoid the black ones.

The assets

At first, let's create our assets. We will need a 50x100 pixels character, a 50x50 red ball, a 50x50 black ball, and a "Game Over" one.

Here are some simple examples for the graphics:

1. **The guy:**

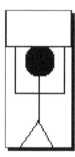

2. **The bomb:**

3. **The tomato:**

That leaves us with the following XML to be given to SWFMILL:

```xml
<?xml version="1.0" encoding="utf-8"?>
<movie width="60" height="20" framerate="20"
  frames="1" as3="1" version="9">
<frame>
<library>
        <clip id="Guy" import="image/guy.png"/>
        <clip id="Bomb" import="image/bomb.png"/>
        <clip id="Tomato" import="image/tomato.png"/>
        <clip id="Gameover" import="image/gameover.png"/>
</library>
</frame>
</movie>
```

 Note that I have decided that red balls are tomatoes and black ones are bombs. Both of them will be "Droppable" and therefore, will inherit from "Droppable" for typing purpose.

At the end, we should get something that looks similar to the following image:

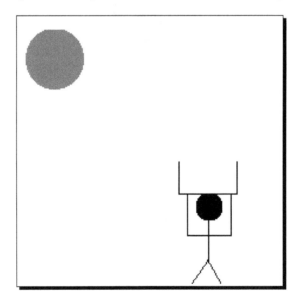

Here is the code for Guy.hx:

```haxe
import flash.display.MovieClip;
@:bind class Guy extends MovieClip
{
```

```
    public function new()
    {
        super();
    }
}
```

Droppable.hx:

```
class Droppable extends flash.display.MovieClip
{
    public function new()
    {
        super();
    }
}
```

Bomb.hx:

```
@:bind class Bomb extends Droppable
{
    public function new()
    {
        super();
    }
}
```

Tomato.hx:

```
@:bind class Tomato extends Droppable
{
    public function new()
    {
        super();
    }
}
```

In addition, Gameover.hx:

```
@:bind class Gameover extends flash.display.MovieClip
{
    public function new()
    {
        super();
    }
}
```

The player's character

Now, let's create the player's character. We will do that in the following two steps:

- In the first step, we will draw it on the screen
- In the second step, we will handle moves

Time for action – Drawing the character

In order to draw our character on the screen, we will simply have to create an instance of the Guy class and add it to the stage.

We will also, as there is only one instance of it, store it as a static variable of our main class. So, here is our Game.hx file:

```
class Game
{
   static var player : Guy;

   public static function main(): Void
   {
      player = new Guy();
      //Add it to the stage
      flash.Lib.current.stage.addChild(player);

      //Place it at the good place on stage.
      player.x = 200;
      player.y = 300;
      player.width=50;
      player.height = 100;
   }
}
```

Time for action – Handling moves

Now, we will add a function that allows the user to control his character.

To do so, we need to listen for when a key is pressed to set the speed of the character, and for when a key is depressed in order to set the speed to 0.

We will also store the speed as a static variable:

```
class Game
{
   static var player : Guy;
   static var horizontalSpeed : Int = 0;

   public static function main(): Void
   {
      player = new Guy();
      //Add it to the stage
      flash.Lib.current.stage.addChild(player);

      //Place it at the good place on stage.
      player.x = 200;
      player.y = 300;
      player.width=50;
      player.height = 100;

      flash.Lib.current.stage.addEventListener
         (flash.events.KeyboardEvent.KEY_DOWN, keyDown);
      flash.Lib.current.stage.addEventListener
         (flash.events.KeyboardEvent.KEY_UP, keyUp);
   }

   private static function keyDown(args : flash.events.KeyboardEvent)
   {
      trace(args.keyCode);
      switch(args.keyCode)
      {
         case 37: //Left
            trace("Left");
            horizontalSpeed = -10;
         case 39: //Right
            trace("Right");
            horizontalSpeed = 10;
      }
   }

   private static function keyUp(args : flash.events.KeyboardEvent)
   {
      trace(args.keyCode);
      switch(args.keyCode)
      {
         case 37: //Left
```

```
        trace("Left");
        horizontalSpeed = 0;
      case 39: //Right
        trace("Right");
        horizontalSpeed = 0;
    }
  }


}
```

What just happened?

Now, the user can set the movement of the character, but it won't really move since we never changed the coordinates of `player`.

Time for action – Moving the character

In order to do so, we are going to await the `ENTER_FRAME` event that is triggered every time a new frame is drawn on the screen (frame drawing is automatically handled in Flash and you do not have to handle it through a loop like in other languages).

We will then move the character on each frame depending on its speed. Let's add the following to the `Game` class:

```
import flash.events.Event;

class Game
{
  //previous code
  public static function main(): Void
  {
    //previous code
    //Add an event handler for every frame drawing
      flash.Lib.current.stage.addEventListener
        (flash.events.Event.ENTER_FRAME, enterFrame);
  }

  //previous code
  private static function enterFrame(args : Dynamic)
  {
    player.x += horizontalSpeed;
  }
}
```

What just happened?

With this code, the character will move on each frame depending on its speed.

Time for action – Adding balls

Now, let's add some falling "balls".

In order to do this, we will create a static list of droppables that we will keep updated (adding newly created ones and removing those that are not used anymore).

We will also use a `haxe.Timer` to regularly create a new droppable. Reference to this timer will be held in a static variable.

We will update droppables' position on each frame.

So, let's create our timer in our `main` function and use an anonymous function to create our new droppable:

```
public static function main(): Void
{
    player = new Guy();
    //Add it to the stage
    flash.Lib.current.stage.addChild(player);

    //Place it at the good place on stage.
    player.x = 200;
    player.y = 300;
    player.width=50;
    player.height = 100;

    flash.Lib.current.stage.addEventListener
        (flash.events.KeyboardEvent.KEY_DOWN, keyDown);
    flash.Lib.current.stage.addEventListener
        (flash.events.KeyboardEvent.KEY_UP, keyUp);
    flash.Lib.current.stage.addEventListener
        (flash.events.Event.ENTER_FRAME, enterFrame);

    timer = new haxe.Timer(750);
    timer.run = function()
    {
        var newDroppable : Droppable;
        if(Math.random() >= 0.75)
        {
            newDroppable = new Bomb();
        } else
```

```
        {
            newDroppable = new Tomato();
        }
        droppables.add(newDroppable);
        newDroppable.x = Math.random() * 400;
        newDroppable.y = -50;
        flash.Lib.current.stage.addChild(newDroppable);
    }
}
```

What just happened?

This is a pretty easy one. We just create a new droppable (randomly a tomato or a bomb) every 750 ms.

Time for action – Updating the position

Now, let's update the positions at every frame. To do that, we will create a simple function and call it in our ENTER_FRAME event handler as follows:

```
private static function enterFrame(args : Dynamic)
{
    player.x += horizontalSpeed;
    updatePositions();
}

private static function updatePositions()
{
    for(d in droppables)
    {
        d.y += 10;
        if(d.y>= 450)
        {
            droppables.remove(d);
            flash.Lib.current.stage.removeChild(d);
            continue;
        }
    }
}
```

What just happened?

This is a pretty simple modification that just updates the position of every droppable and tests whether it is out of the stage or not. If it is, it then removes it from the list of droppables.

That's fine, but we still need the collision detection in order to know if our player touches a tomato or a bomb.

Time for action – Detecting collisions

We will use the `hitTestObject` function that every display object has. It allows one to test if two display objects are colliding (this is based on the bounds of these objects, so if you are looking for something that's pixel perfect, then you should use something else.)

```
private static function updatePositions()
{
    for(d in droppables)
    {
        d.y += 10;
        if(d.y>= 450)
        {
            droppables.remove(d);
            flash.Lib.current.stage.removeChild(d);
            continue;
        }
        //Test for collisions
        if(player.hitTestObject(d))
        {
            if(Std.is(d, Bomb))
            {
                trace("GAME OVER");
                timer.stop();
                var go = new Gameover();
                go.x = 0;
                go.y = 150;
                flash.Lib.current.stage.addChild(go);
            } else
            {
                trace("Score + 1");
                droppables.remove(d);
                flash.Lib.current.stage.removeChild(d);
            }
        }
    }
}
```

What just happened?

As we only have one list of droppables, we want to know if it is a bomb or a tomato and in order to know that, we use `Std.is`. This is certainly not the best option in terms of performances, but as we do not have many collisions happening, this is fine in our case.

Therefore, we now have the following class:

```
import flash.events.Event;

class Game
{
    static var player : Guy;
    static var horizontalSpeed : Int = 0;
    //Stores droppables that are on-screen
    static var droppables : List<Droppable> = new List<Droppable>();
    //Used to generate droppables
    static var timer : haxe.Timer;

    public static function main(): Void
    {
        player = new Guy();
        //Add it to the stage
        flash.Lib.current.stage.addChild(player);

        //Place it at the good place on stage.
        player.x = 200;
        player.y = 300;
        player.width=50;
        player.height = 100;

        flash.Lib.current.stage.addEventListener
          (flash.events.KeyboardEvent.KEY_DOWN, keyDown);
        flash.Lib.current.stage.addEventListener
          (flash.events.KeyboardEvent.KEY_UP, keyUp);
        flash.Lib.current.stage.addEventListener
          (flash.events.Event.ENTER_FRAME, enterFrame);

        timer = new haxe.Timer(750);
        timer.run = function()
        {
            var newDroppable : Droppable;
            if(Math.random() >= 0.75)
            {
                newDroppable = new Bomb();
```

```
    } else
    {
       newDroppable = new Tomato();
    }
    droppables.add(newDroppable);
    newDroppable.x = Math.random() * 400;
    newDroppable.y = -50;
    flash.Lib.current.stage.addChild(newDroppable);
  }
}

private static function keyDown(args : flash.events.KeyboardEvent)
{
  trace(args.keyCode);
  switch(args.keyCode)
  {
     case 37: //Left
        trace("Left");
        horizontalSpeed = -10;
     case 39: //Right
        trace("Right");
        horizontalSpeed = 10;
  }
}

private static function keyUp(args : flash.events.KeyboardEvent)
{
  trace(args.keyCode);
  switch(args.keyCode)
  {
     case 37: //Left
        trace("Left");
        horizontalSpeed = 0;
     case 39: //Right
        trace("Right");
        horizontalSpeed = 0;
  }
}

private static function enterFrame(args : Dynamic)
{
  player.x += horizontalSpeed;
  updatePositions();
}
```

```
private static function updatePositions()
{
    for(d in droppables)
    {
        d.y += 10;
        if(d.y>= 450)
        {
            droppables.remove(d);
            flash.Lib.current.stage.removeChild(d);
            continue;
        }
        //Test for collisions
        if(player.hitTestObject(d))
        {
            if(Std.is(d, Bomb))
            {
                trace("GAME OVER");
                timer.stop();
                var go = new Gameover();
                go.x = 0;
                go.y = 150;
                flash.Lib.current.stage.addChild(go);
            } else
            {
                trace("Score + 1");
                droppables.remove(d);
                flash.Lib.current.stage.removeChild(d);
            }
        }
    }
}
```

With this class, we now have our game completed!

If you want to go further, you could try to improve it (for example) by adding some animations to it.

Have a go hero – Adding a proper score display

At the moment, we simply use a trace function to display the player's score. You could try to improve it by adding a counter in the top-right corner.

Have a go hero – Adding an online score table

Try to implement a server to store scores online. This could be done using haXe Remoting.

Pop quiz – Software used

1. The software we used in this chapter to embed assets is:

    a. SWFMILL

    b. The haXe compiler

    c. We just have to create an XML file

Summary

In this chapter, we have seen how to embed and use assets. We have also seen how one may use Flash's events system.

Moreover, we have written a simple game that should help you understand how to get started with Flash game programming using haXe.

Specifically, we covered how to embed assets in a SWF file, how to use them, and how to handle events.

I hope this book has been a good introduction to haXe for you. You should now be able to write your own haXe applications and continue learning how to work with haXe.

This programming language is very powerful and lets you write code in several different ways.

Do not forget that haXe is driven by its community and that a lot of code is open source, letting you dive into it to learn how others are using haXe and how they write their own code.

Pop Quiz Answers

Chapter 1: Getting to know haXe

1	a, b, and c
2	b
3	a
4	c

Chapter 3: Being Cross-platform with haXe

1	a
2	c

Chapter 4: Understanding Types

1	a
2	a
3	a and b
4	d
5	b

Chapter 5: The Dynamic Type and Properties

1	b
2	a

Chapter 6: Using and Writing Interfaces, Typedefs, and Enums

1	c
2	d
3	a

Chapter 7: Communication Between haXe Programs

1	a
2	c

Chapter 8: Accessing Databases

1	a
2	b

Chapter 9: Templating

1	b
2	a

Chapter 10: Interfacing with the Target Platform

1	b
2	a
3	a

Chapter 12: Creating a Game with haXe and Flash

1	a

Index

Run Time Type Information. *See* RTTI

S

safe casting
  performing 88
sayHello method 50
sayHiTo function 117
screen
  character, drawing on 242
search function 165
setter
  writing 107, 108
shift method 89
Simple Persistence Objects Database. *See* SPOD
socket option 157
sound tag 237
SPOD
  about 159
  cache system 161
  connection, initiating to database 162-164
  example 161
  not-mapped fields 160, 161
  table name 160
SPOD class
  creating 190, 191
SPOD object
  setting 159, 160
SPOD system
  database, connecting to 191, 192
sponsor property 166
SQLite databases
  about 154
  connecting to 157
SQL usage 154
standard input interface 62
standard library
  about 55
  object storage 56
standard output interface 62
static typing 74
static variables 36
Std class 56
stderr 62
stdin 62
stdout 62
StorableIterator class 130

storedOn property 128
strings, haXe constant 29, 30
Sub-Templates
  integrating 189
SWF file
  creating 236
SWFMILL
  about 236
  installing 236
  library, creating with 236
  SWF file, creating with 236
switch construct
  about 42
  example 42
switch keyword 42

T

TABLE_NAME variable 160
tar -zxf hxinst-linux.tgz command 17
template
  creating 192, 193
  executing 194-196
template engine, haXe
  arrays, using 184-187
  iterables, using 184-187
  lists, using 184-187
template.execute function 187
template macros 187
templates
  about 181
  benefits 182
  haXe code, executing from 187-189
  reading, from resources 193, 194
TextMate 18
texts 216
this keyword 39, 218
title field 169
toLowerCas function 32
trace method 20, 22
try keyword 48
typed container
  creating 93
typedefs, haXe
  about 116
  anonymous types, naming 116, 117
  duck typing 120, 121

Thank you for buying
haXe 2 Beginner's Guide

About Packt Publishing

Packt, pronounced 'packed', published its first book "*Mastering phpMyAdmin for Effective MySQL Management*" in April 2004 and subsequently continued to specialize in publishing highly focused books on specific technologies and solutions.

Our books and publications share the experiences of your fellow IT professionals in adapting and customizing today's systems, applications, and frameworks. Our solution based books give you the knowledge and power to customize the software and technologies you're using to get the job done. Packt books are more specific and less general than the IT books you have seen in the past. Our unique business model allows us to bring you more focused information, giving you more of what you need to know, and less of what you don't.

Packt is a modern, yet unique publishing company, which focuses on producing quality, cutting-edge books for communities of developers, administrators, and newbies alike. For more information, please visit our website: www.packtpub.com.

About Packt Open Source

In 2010, Packt launched two new brands, Packt Open Source and Packt Enterprise, in order to continue its focus on specialization. This book is part of the Packt Open Source brand, home to books published on software built around Open Source licences, and offering information to anybody from advanced developers to budding web designers. The Open Source brand also runs Packt's Open Source Royalty Scheme, by which Packt gives a royalty to each Open Source project about whose software a book is sold.

Writing for Packt

We welcome all inquiries from people who are interested in authoring. Book proposals should be sent to author@packtpub.com. If your book idea is still at an early stage and you would like to discuss it first before writing a formal book proposal, contact us; one of our commissioning editors will get in touch with you.

We're not just looking for published authors; if you have strong technical skills but no writing experience, our experienced editors can help you develop a writing career, or simply get some additional reward for your expertise.

Flash Game Development by Example

ISBN: 978-1-849690-90-4   Paperback: 328 pages

Build 10 classic Flash games and learn game development along the way

1. Build 10 classic games in Flash. Learn the essential skills for Flash game development.

2. Start developing games straight away. Build your first game in the first chapter.

3. Fun and fast paced. Ideal for readers with no Flash or game programming experience.Topic

4. The most popular games in the world are built in Flash.

Python 3 Object Oriented Programming

ISBN: 978-1-849511-26-1   Paperback: 404 pages

Harness the power of Python 3 objects

1. Learn how to do Object Oriented Programming in Python using this step-by-step tutorial

2. Design public interfaces using abstraction, encapsulation, and information hiding

3. Turn your designs into working software by studying the Python syntax

4. Raise, handle, define, and manipulate exceptions using special error objects

5. Implement Object Oriented Programming in Python using practical examples

Please check **www.PacktPub.com** for information on our titles

Python Testing: Beginner's Guide

ISBN: 978-1-847198-84-6   Paperback: 256 pages

An easy and convenient approach to testing your powerful Python projects

1. Covers everything you need to test your code in Python

2. Easiest and enjoyable approach to learn Python testing

3. Write, execute, and understand the result of tests in the unit test framework

4. Packed with step-by-step examples and clear explanations

Python 3 Web Development Beginner's Guide

ISBN: 978-1-849513-74-6   Paperback: 336 pages

Use Python to create, theme, and deploy unique web applications

1. Build your own Python web applications from scratch

2. Follow the examples to create a number of different Python-based web applications, including a task list, book database, and wiki application

3. Have the freedom to make your site your own without having to learn another framework

4. Part of Packt's Beginner's Guide Series: practical examples will make it easier for you to get going quickly

Please check **www.PacktPub.com** for information on our titles

www.ingramcontent.com/pod-product-compliance
Lightning Source LLC
Chambersburg PA
CBHW060522060326
40690CB00017B/3353